Schooling Horses In Hand

A Means of Suppling and Collection

Richard Hinrichs

Schooling Horses In Hand
A Means of Suppling and Collection

J. A. Allen
London

Published in Great Britain in 2001 by
J.A. Allen
an imprint of Robert Hale Ltd.
Clerkenwell House
45-47 Clerkenwell Green
London EC1R 0HT

Printed in Hong Kong

Originally published in the German language as *Pferde schulen an der Hand* by Franckh-Kosmos Verlags-GmbH & Co., Stuttgart, 1999.

Photos and illustrations by Gerhard Kapitzke throughout, as well as an illustration by Heinz-Peter Brust (p. 34); a photo by Ursula Bruns (p. 147); a photo by Marian Forrer (p.111); four photos by Guido Giffels (pp. 87, 93 bottom, 150, 151 top); a photo by Gabriele Kottlorz (p. 103 left); a photo by Jeanine Krämer (pp. 14-15); a photo by Sabine Küpper (p. 102), a photo by Nicole Sachs (p. 154); and four photos by Walburga Schmidt (pp. 11, 143, 151 bottom, 152 top).

ISBN: 0.85131.834.7

British Library Cataloguing in Publication Data
A catalogue record for this book is available from the British Library

Jacket design: Judy Linard
Typeface: Janson Text and Ex Ponto by Adobe

Table of Contents

Part Four
Airs Above the Ground 139

Foreword

The art of riding gradually evolved as human beings thought more about their interaction with the horse. In the beginning, a fairly modest method of training was enough to make the horse a hunting or fighting companion. But equitation demands a much higher human application in order to enlist the horse's psyche to the service to the human being.

As in many other arts, the ability to do this was restricted to particularly sensitive individuals who were able to gain access to the horse's psyche. It is thanks to these people that today we possess such a valuable collection of communication possibilities, which are able to replace spoken language. The better people can communicate with the horse, the greater his artistic possibilities, and the more expressive the combination of horse and rider will appear.

If, in the course of centuries, these talented people had not tried and tested such valuable methods and passed them on to us, the state of training horses today would indeed be meager. Current generations certainly have a good command of technology in many areas. However, in the field of communication with the horse, no progress whatsoever has been made. In his book Schooling Horses In-hand, Richard Hinrichs has shown, in a way that is particularly helpful to people wishing to learn the methods of classical schooling, how to achieve this higher level of communication. He has also included "airs above the ground" such as the levade, courbette, and capriole. Today, these movements are rarely found in an instructional book. We should be very grateful to the author for including these subjects here.

Perhaps a number of readers may be of the opinion that some of the subject matter included is superfluous because breeding has already made such an excellent equine partner available to the human being and extra human brain work is unnecessary. People of such opinion should, however, remember that even today the "thinking rider" still remains superior to the rider who does not apply his mind to the task.

If the author has also managed to help people overcome their shyness in dealing with the term "classical equitation" and, in this way, helped them to find the key to the horse's psyche, then yet another aim will have been achieved. Today more than ever, we need people to interpret and help us to translate this valuable inheritance into our present day language and to fit it into the training routine. We should gratefully accept this gift and do everything we can to use the talents that nature has provided in order to make the horse into a true partner of the human being.

In his book, the author has included much valuable theoretical knowledge that has also been well tried in practice. The book is not only worthwhile for purposes of study and expanding knowledge, but it is also a source that we can use with great pleasure to achieve happiness as riders. It deserves to become a valuable part of present day equestrian literature. Let us hope that equitation will follow the lead that the author has outlined for us.

Brigadier Professor Kurt Albrecht

Professor Albrecht was director of the Spanish Riding School in Vienna from 1974 to 1985. As an equestrian expert of the highest level, he is much in demand today as an international judge and trainer, and as a tireless supporter of the classical values of equitation.

Introduction

It is certainly a somewhat unorthodox approach to first produce an instructional videotape, and subsequently to write a book on the subject, as is the case here. The idea for the video, Schooling Horses in Hand, came first, and it was made available by Trafalgar Square Publishing. While formulating the script, it became clear that many aspects that are significant for success, or lack of it, when working with the horse without the rider's weight, can be only generally outlined in a 45-minute video. Unfortunately it is not possible to comment on them in detail in that amount of time.

Many people who have seen the video have suggested that a book should follow. It is now being presented here, in the hope that the additional explanations will make it easier for the reader to fully explore the possibilities of training a horse in hand.

COMMUNICATION WITHOUT THE RIDER'S WEIGHT

There are many reasons for working a horse in hand without the stress of the rider's weight. Work in hand can be used to prepare and also complement the horse's work under the rider. Trust and confidence in the trainer, as well as obedience toward him, can be developed in hand and have a very favorable effect later when new demands are placed on the horse.

This book is intended to demonstrate certain set patterns in equine behavior. If these are observed and followed appropriately, disturbances in harmony between the human being and the horse can, for the most part, be avoided. The human being/horse relationship functions best when the horse is relaxed, physically and mentally at ease, and well balanced. Work in hand offers some especially effective possibilities to create this situation. For example, in nature a horse holds his head and neck in a high position when he is physically excited, while a relaxed horse keeps his head lowered. In order to physically and mentally relax a horse that is physically and mentally excited, we must encourage him to stretch his head forward and downward. As a result of the change in body posture, a change occurs in his mental state. The horse relaxes. It makes sense, therefore, to relax the young horse without the extra stress of the rider's weight, which might actually increase the physical and mental strain.

1 *Richard Hinrichs on the Friesian stallion, Nardo.*

There are some very competent riders who have observed that young horses relax faster under the rider than they do in hand. This is usually because the rider's mounted technique is better developed than his ability to influence the horse's behavior from the ground. This book is intended to offer assistance in training without the rider's weight in a way that is kind to horses. This offers considerable advantages, particularly in the case of horses that cannot take too much strain. A trainer who is in a position to use a wide range of methods with a gentle effect on horses will always be in a superior position to someone who can only apply his abilities if he has high-quality horse "material" available.

WAYS TO RELAX AND COLLECT

Work in hand helps a horse to gain trust and confidence in his trainer, to develop obedience toward him, and to relax. It also makes it possible to collect the horse well without the rider's weight. This prepares the horse for and encourages collection under the rider. In classical collection it is described as balance of the horse over a small surface of support. A horse is collected when his hind legs come in close to the forelegs, take up an increasing amount of weight, and thus relieve the forelegs. In nature, the position of the neck and head of the horse means that the forelegs bear considerably more weight than the hind legs. The addition of the rider's weight can, then, mean considerable stress. The shifting of weight caused by collection will reduce wear and tear on the horse.

Furthermore, the collected horse reacts better to more subtle aids than the horse that is not collected. Many horses find finer, subtler aids more pleasant than rougher ones and consequently continue to respond to them even when they are not actually collected. Thus, collection is a means by

2 Maestoso Gratia in piaffe, at the Herrenhaus Gardens, Hannover.

3 *The Lusitano stallion, Girassol: in the pesade in long reins.*

which to condition the horse to a finer application of the aids. Under certain conditions, collecting exercises can also have a suppling-up effect. I shall talk more about this later.

SENSITIVITY TRAINING FOR THE RIDER

The intention of this book is to show how the use of reins, whip, voice, and body language can encourage voluntary co-operation of the horse without the rider's weight. I will refer repeatedly to the requirements under the rider because the work in hand without the rider's weight is not an aim in itself. It can prepare and complement the work under the rider, and is an excellent way of training the rider's sensitivity. It is, however, not a method by which all problems can be solved; in particular, it does not take away from the reader the task of actually learning to ride, of constantly striving for a correct seat, and of coordinating his own movements as well as his general effect on the horse. The book can indeed provide useful guidance, however, it by no means replaces regular control by a qualified instructor. Videotapes for self-monitoring purposes can also be helpful in recognizing serious mistakes— and then avoiding them afterward. Anyone who does not achieve his aim straight away should not be discouraged. Learning is a constant process.

Longeing a riding horse has many purposes, such as preparing a young horse for work under saddle, carefully suppling-up the advanced horse, and maintaining fitness.

Another useful aspect of longeing is to improve the rider's seat, although this aspect is not treated in detail here, as it would go beyond the scope set for this book.

PART ONE

Longeing

Equipment and Auxiliary Aids

4 Longeing provides useful assistance to the rider in practicing sitting exercises. A prerequisite for this is that the horse reacts willingly to the trainer's aids.

Anyone who wants to become actively involved with longeing must have the necessary equipment. The most important components are listed here, together with some brief notes on the subject.

LONGE LINE

The longe line should be at least 20-feet (7 m) long and comfortable to hold—not too heavy and able to move easily through the holder's fingers. Webbing longe lines are preferable to longe lines made of nylon, which slip too easily through the holder's hand if a disobedient horse reacts in an unexpectedly headstrong way.

I do not recommend longe lines with stoppers. Anyone who feels comfortable with these longe lines usually longes in such a way that the horse has a strong contact with the hand that is too strong. In such situations, the stoppers prevent the longe from slipping through the hand, giving the person holding the line a false feeling of security. A more flexible hold is better.

The longe line should be arranged in neat loops so that it can be easily shortened or lengthened to any extent and at any time (fig. 5).

5 A longe line correctly held. It is a good idea to always wear gloves when longeing.

THE CAVESSON

The longeing cavesson should be as light as possible and not too heavily padded in the nose area under the metal plate. Few commercially available cavessons fulfill these requirements. Instead they are usually heavy, awkward to use and, as a result of heavy padding in the nose area, almost ineffective and therefore not particularly pleasant either for trainer or horse.

The heavy cavessons, some of them with two throat latches and a superfluous strap running vertically from the middle of the noseband up between the ears of the horse through to the headpiece, have done much to increase the aversion of many riders to this instrument. Look for a light cavesson with cheekpieces going fairly far back so that even if the horse gives a short pull on the longe, the outside cheekpiece is not pulled over the horse's outside eye. The cheekpieces should also be attached underneath the horse's chin groove by means of a firmly fixed cross strap (figs. 6 and 7).

The cavesson described here makes a clear influence on the horse's nose possible, which means that he can be disciplined when being led. It can be used for leading, longeing, and for suppling-up and collecting exercises in hand. In addition, it can

6 A light cavesson, without unnecessary padding, is best.

also be helpful when breaking in younger horses that tend to go behind the bit. Directing a horse with a line attached to the cavesson instead of to a bit and bridle at this stage will avoid the undesirable reaction of going behind the bit. The bit and bridge can be added gradually later. It is usually best to attach the leading rein or the longe line to the ring on the cavesson on the side where the trainer is walking so that the cavesson will not be pulled crooked on the horse's head if he moves suddenly. However, if this position of the leading rein or the longe line seems uncomfortable, particularly in the case of a young horse, try the middle ring.

7 A light cavesson (Viennese model).

THE BRIDLE

I will be discussing the use of side reins and draw reins in longeing, but before the horse has auxiliary reins attached on the side for longeing, he should already be used to the bridle. I recommend the full-cheek snaffle bit for the young horse (fig. 8). It is used in the Spanish Riding School in Vienna and has the advantage that, when correctly fitted, it prevents any excess tongue play, and therefore tongue faults of the horse (such as putting the tongue over the bit). The two metal bars of the bit outside the horse's mouth must be attached vertically to the bridle's cheek-pieces to achieve the desired effect (fig. 8A).

It is possible to pervert any good principle if it is used for a purpose for which it was never intended.

In the case of particularly sensitive horses, I recommend using a double-jointed bit such as a French link, which, by contrast to the usual bits with a single break, does not exert pressure on the joint under the tongue even when the reins are pulled tightly (figs. 8 B and C). Plastic bits are also worth considering for such horses.

More important than the material is that the mouthpiece fits well into the mouth of the horse and does not provoke resistance. In Germany, many riders are of the opinion that a thick snaffle is the most pleasant bit for the horse with the gentlest effect. However, this is not true if the bit is so thick that the horse can hardly close his mouth, or not close it at all. Any good principle can be perverted if it is not applied for the correct purpose. Many styles of bridle can be used, as long as they do not restrict the horse's breathing.

When longeing, the bridle is used in addition to the cavesson if the horse is to work in auxiliary reins. If you attach auxiliary reins laterally to the cavesson you may bring the horse's head into the desired position, but this does not prepare the horse for halts, which the horse must feel on his mouth. This can only be achieved if the auxiliary reins are attached to the snaffle bit.

In the Spanish Riding School in Vienna, and Iberian countries generally, the longe line is not attached to the snaffle but rather to the cavesson. In Germany, by contrast, it is common to longe the horse with the longe line directly attached to the snaffle.

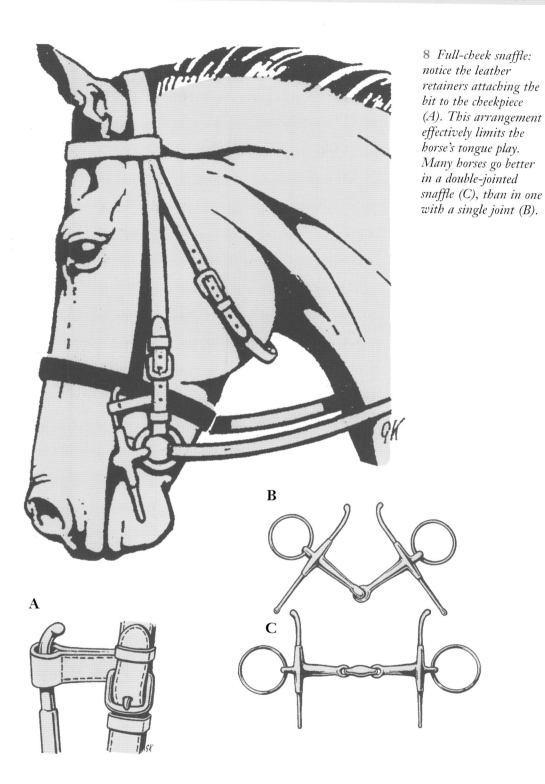

8 *Full-cheek snaffle: notice the leather retainers attaching the bit to the cheekpiece (A). This arrangement effectively limits the horse's tongue play. Many horses go better in a double-jointed snaffle (C), than in one with a single joint (B).*

B

A

C

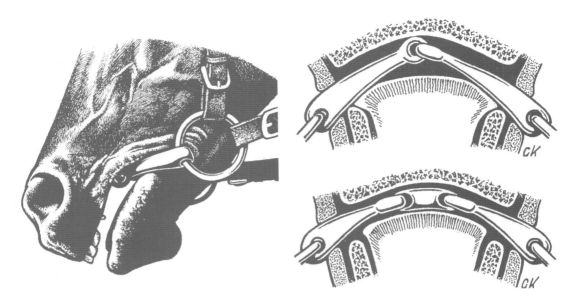

9 *Above and top right: a single-jointed snaffle with pinching effect on the lower jaw and pressure against the tongue. Bottom right: a double-jointed snaffle bit and its position in the horse's mouth.*

In the case of older, and more experienced horses, the cavesson may be dispensed with, if the horse is well behaved. In the case of young horses, however, it is always quite possible that, in an outbreak of high spirits, they may suddenly pull too strongly on the longe or have to be disciplined by means of the longe line. In these situations the sensitivity of the horse's mouth can be preserved better if the longe line is attached to the cavesson rather than the snaffle.

SIDE REINS AND DRAW REINS

Side reins should be made of strong material (I prefer leather). Rubber rings are not always a good feature because they can cause some horses to keep trying out the yielding capacity of the side reins and thus to fight against the strict limits they impose.

The drawing on page 23 shows how the side reins work. Imagine the point at which the side reins are attached to the girth as the center of a circle. The snaffle ring to which the other end of the side reins is attached forms a part of the circle outline when the horse straightens up more or holds his head lower. Thus the horse's neck can stretch best when the side reins run horizontally (fig. 10). If the side reins are taut and the horse holds his head in a higher or lower position so that the side reins run in an upward or downward direction, the neck contracts and the horse feels clear muscular tension. Since the horse feels more comfortable with relaxed neck muscles than with tense ones, use this connection to bring the horse's head into the desired position.

If you want a higher position of the horse's head, then attach the side reins correspondingly high. If you want the horse to stretch well forward and downward without bringing his nose behind the vertical, then attach the side reins lower.

In order to achieve the desired effect, the trainer has to prepare his horse in such a way that the horse does not resent

10 *A horse wearing side reins.*

11 *The limiting effect of side reins.*

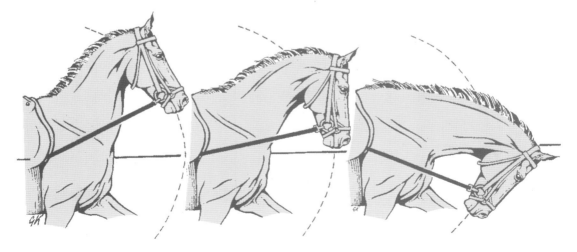

the side reins but rather accepts them without tension. We will see how to achieve this in connection with longeing the young horse.

Particularly fine and sensitive horses that do not stretch trustingly into tight side reins should be worked with draw reins. Depending on whether the forward and downward stretching of the head and neck section or lateral flexibility has priority, the draw reins can be attached accordingly (see figs. 12 and 13).

Whether or not a horse wears auxiliary reins such as side or draw reins for work in hand depends on the individual. Normally the use of auxiliary reins fulfills a useful purpose, but in individual cases it is dependent on the character of the horse and the abilities of the trainer. Many horses can be brought on better in hand with auxiliary reins than without them. For particularly sensitive horses draw reins are usually better because they are less restricting than the firm side reins. The draw reins can be attached in different ways according to the training goal.

12　The method of attaching draw reins that encourages a stretching posture.

THE ROLLER AND THE SADDLE

A roller should have a lot of side rings, which permit attachment of auxiliary reins and lines at different heights according to need. The rings in the lower area are particularly important. If they are used to attach the side reins a horse that is already used to them can be encouraged to hold his head low. If he raises his head with taut side reins the contact becomes stronger and therefore also the pressure of the bit on the horse's tongue and sides of the mouth. If the horse is relaxed enough, he will bring his head down again in order to avoid the pressure. As already mentioned, the horse can only stretch his neck forward and downward the way we want him to when the side reins are attached in a low position. When they are attached higher, the horse contracts his neck when he lowers his head and his nose drops behind the vertical where it doesn't belong. A horse's frame can vary considerably depending on whether the auxiliary reins are attached a few inches or centimeters higher or lower. For this reason it should be emphasized once again that having many rings in the lower area of the roller is particularly important.

13 *These draw reins are attached in a manner that place the horse's head in the desired position.*

If the horse is used to a roller, he can also be longed with a saddle. The side reins can be attached to the girth. If you want to be more precise about the height of the reins, put a roller over the saddle so that the side reins can be brought through the rings.

The Longe Whip

The longeing whip should be as light as possible. Even very slight weight differences can have a considerable effect when longeing over a lengthy period of time. The thin leather strap attached to the whip should be long enough to be able to touch the horse without any major physical contortions on the part of the trainer. At the end of the leather strap there should be a short whip lash of natural fiber to make cracking the whip easier.

When buying a longeing whip, an inexperienced person should try holding several different whips in his hand in order to test their weight and flexibility. Choose a whip that is com-

14 *How to limit the size of a circle when longeing a young horse in a riding arena.*

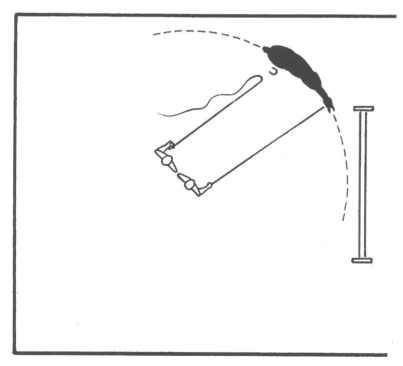

fortable to hold, so that the movement of the lash is easy to direct. The material the whip is made of is not particularly important. Whips should be treated with the utmost of care—stood up, hung up, or laid down so that they stay straight and do not become warped. In my experience, whips made of wood are particularly prone to warping. If you choose a whip made of wood, take great care to ensure that it remains straight.

15 While longeing, it is important to have the right equipment in order to create a pleasant working atmosphere.

GLOVES

Young horses, and those that are not used to working on the longe, may pull the longe line through the trainer's hand, causing injury to unprotected hands. Always wear gloves when longeing.

Choose gloves that are made of a material that is strong enough to withstand the rubbing of the longe line and reins. At the same time, however, they should not be so thick that they interfere with the gentle opening and closing of the hand—an action similar to wringing out a sponge—that the horse will learn to obey.

Longeing a Young Horse

On the longe line a young horse can be prepared carefully and kindly—without the rider's weight—for later work under the rider, and the horse can be relaxed in a particularly effective way. Trust in the trainer and the necessary obedience toward him can be built up, creating an optimum atmosphere for further training.

A young horse must lead well before he is longed. Leading on a cavesson, as compared with leading on a halter, has the advantage that the horse learns to respect half-halts (very short, clear rein pulls followed by yielding) right from the very beginning. Also, the trainer does not need to apply as much physical force with a cavesson as when leading with a halter, so the horse can immediately become accustomed to the authority of the trainer.

Once the horse is obedient when being led, get the horse used to moving in a circle if you can use a fenced-in longeing circle. If one of these is not available, it is possible to close off the end of an arena with poles or cavaletti laid perpendicular to the long side (fig. 14).

16 An assistant is leading the young horse on the circle.

LONGEING WITH AN ASSISTANT

At the beginning it is always helpful if two people are available to longe: an assistant leads the horse in the cavesson on the circle so the horse becomes accustomed to it. After a short time the helper can then go into the middle of the circle and help to guide the longeing from there while the trainer keeps the horse moving forward with the whip. With this allocation of tasks, the assistant can soon turn on his inner heel and thus prescribe exactly the center point of the circle. The trainer, who can then move about freely, can drive with the whip so the horse cannot turn around or avoid moving forward on the circle in other ways.

APPLICATIONS OF THE AIDS

Use of subtle gestures, even at this early stage of training, helps to increase the trainer's authority. A command—initially with the voice—should, if it is not responded to, be followed up by an effective driving or restraining aid, such as the whip or pressure from the longe line. The horse will soon understand that politeness—the friendly voice aid—is not to be understood as weakness.

Note that voice and whip aids should not be given simultaneously when longeing. Instead, the voice should be used shortly before the movement of the whip or touching with the whiplash. If the horse learns that the voice is just the beginning of all possible actions, and some of the next ones could possibly have unpleasant effects, he will react promptly to the voice aid and not wait for further measures from the trainer.

The element of surprise is important here. For example, the trainer should not swing the whiplash from a full-arm extension so the horse can see it coming. Rather the end of the whiplash should go out

17 Longeing the young horse, with a helper ready to assist, if needed.

to the horse as a result of a small powerful movement of the wrist, ideally without any noticeable movement of the whip stick.

The horse must have the impression that the trainer can always apply the aids with more force if he chooses. The trainer can do this only if he starts with a small amount of force and builds from there.

The basic position of the tip of the longeing whip, for example, should be approximately 8 inches (20 cm) above the ground, so that the horse sees the simple raising of the tip of the whip as a reinforced driving aid. Then, if the horse does not react to this movement, he will pay particular attention to the whip being taken back if this sometimes involves a fast pulling forward again in connection with a crack from the whip lash.

The basic position of the tip of the whip should be directed toward the area between the horse's forelegs and the

18 The whip held low in its basic position for longeing with minimal aids.

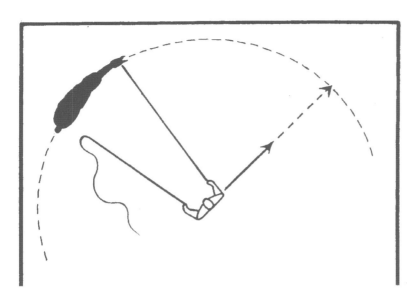

19 *The trainer can "apply the brakes" by moving in front of the horse in the direction of the line of the circle.*

hind legs (fig. 18). Raising the whip and pointing it farther forward can drive the horse out on to a larger circle, and directing the whip farther back will drive him forward more.

During the whole longeing session the whip holder should create the impression that the whip is not an alien item but rather an extension of the trainer's hand. The upper arm, elbow, wrist, and tip of the whip should form an unbroken line. This is easiest to achieve when the hand is slightly turned with the fingernails in an upward position.

In all movements with the whip, the trainer and longe-line holder should remain absolutely vertical and not turn or twist. Otherwise, he does not exude the same confidence and particularly domineering horses would see this as an invitation to dispute the trainer's authority.

Whether the trainer is longeing with an assistant or alone, he should turn or move so that he is always facing squarely toward the middle of the horse. This way the horse comes into his range of vision rather than running out of it. This will prevent the longe handler from becoming dizzy even in the case of fast movement on a small circle. Anyone who becomes dizzy is not going to be capable of giving sufficiently clear instructions to the horse.

The posture of the person longeing the horse is also important. The upper arm should be kept next to the body, while the forearm and the hand holding the longe line form a straight line to the cavesson from the elbow (fig. 18). This position should also be maintained when giving halt aids, so that the angle to the horse remains constant.

The right point in time for the trainer to take over the longe line and whip alone—without an assistant—depends entirely on the horse's progress.

WALKING AND TROTTING PHASES

In the initial phase of longeing it is best to let the horse choose the pace at which he can relax best. For many horses this will be the walk or trot. Generally speaking, the goal should be to begin with the walk as soon as possible and keep the horse at this pace as long as the trainer desires. Some young horses, however, are so tense as a result of the new requirements imposed on them that this tension is increased rather than decreased at a walk.

However, once the horse is confident enough on the longe, insist on beginning the longeing session at a walk. Otherwise the relaxing effect can only take place through tiredness, and in the course of time the horse will constantly develop more stamina—something that is not desirable until the necessary degree of obedience has been achieved.

If the horse trots of his own accord, not in accordance with the trainer's command, and is thus to be brought back to a walk, the longe-line holder may leave his position in the center of the circle and go toward the front of the horse more in order to force him to slow down (fig. 19). In an extreme case, the trainer may stand in the horse's way on the circle and thus force him to stop. Then the next time the longe-line holder moves forward in the direction of the circle, the horse will slow down of his own accord.

CANTERING ON THE LONGE

The horse's character is really the essential factor in deciding when to start cantering work: if the horse is particularly

"If, despite all caution, a horse storms forward, it is better to let him canter on, providing the canter is not too fast, and at the same time to calm him with the voice and, after a certain time, to give the command 'trot' and shake the longe to bring him calmly under control."

Excerpt from the military equestrian publication, *Reitvorschrift*, 1937.

talented, then it is possible to start very early; with a less talented horse it is important to wait much longer.

When cantering a horse on the longe line, be careful not to pull the horse's head over the inside foreleg, because it will put too much strain on the leg and restrict its action. If the inner foreleg cannot stride forward properly, the horse may be forced into a counter or even disunited canter. Instead, with just slight contact, ask the horse to canter as he approaches a fence corner, because this limits the action of the outside foreleg, and the inside foreleg can stride forward. You want the horse to go out of a quiet trot directly into the canter, without extending the trot, so give the aids to canter sharply and clearly.

When giving the command to canter, do not extend the soft "A" vowel sound. This may calm the horse too much and make it more difficult for him to canter off at the precise moment required. Make the command a quick "canter!"

Occasional bucking by the young horse when cantering is to be tolerated, as long as he is generally controllable.

20 The Andalusian stallion, Ureo, at the canter: the side reins are attached relatively low on this horse since he is already accustomed to them. The rubber rings that can be seen here on the side reins are not essential.

SIDE REINS

When the horse accepts the snaffle bridle in addition to the cavesson and the roller or saddle, then work with the side reins can begin.

It is best to allow the young horse to go for a few moments without side reins at the beginning of the training session. In the initial period he will supple up more quickly if the side reins are not attached immediately he comes into the arena.

Begin your work with the side reins very long and not attached too low, so that initially, the horse simply has to become accustomed to them being there. No attempt should be made to shorten the reins until it becomes completely clear that the horse has absolutely no fear of them.

When the side reins are attached low, they exercise more pull and therefore stronger pressure on the tongue and sides of the mouth when the horse straightens up. If the horse is at least reasonably relaxed, they thus encourage the forward and downward stretching of the neck. A very young, inexperienced horse can, however, experience a kind of claustrophobia and panic as a result. He may rear and, in an extreme case, even fall over backward. This is why the side reins should be attached higher initially, even though this high position does not allow a great degree of forward and downward stretching of the neck.

When the horse has become accustomed to the contact with the side reins, they can be attached lower. The goal is to have side reins running more or less horizontally when the horse's head is in the correct position.

STRAIGHTENING THE HORSE'S SPINE

Very few horses are really absolutely straight throughout their whole length from head to tail. Most of them are—to a greater or lesser extent—concave on the left side and convex on the right side. With a small minority of horses, the opposite is true. This natural crookedness is not noticeable in many horses when they are standing, but first becomes recognizable when they are moving.

There are various theories concerning the reason for this crookedness. A commonly held opinion is that it results from the position of the foal in the mare's womb. Just as a human being is either right- or left-handed, a horse is normally better and stronger with one hind leg than the other. Accordingly, one can observe that many horses bring the hip on the side of the weaker hind leg—usually the left—farther forward than on the side of the stronger hind leg, making the left side of the

22 The Lusitano stallion, Xami: cantering on the longe with the left foreleg leading. (The rubber rings on the side reins are not essential here.)

body concave. This makes it less difficult to bring the weaker hind leg forward.

In order to avoid wear and tear as a result of uneven stress on the horse's legs, the horse's spine should be gradually straightened up in the course of training and be exercised and suppled-up in such a way that he actually does go forward in a straight line. With some horses this task is never completed and the problem of crookedness frequently reoccurs whenever a new exercise involves particular physical effort. In every training session then, it is important to find out how the horse's spine can best be straightened.

Begin by positioning and flexing the horse in such a way that the side that was previously concave becomes convex. With increasing elasticity of the horse, his tendency to go crooked decreases accordingly. On the longe, by way of preparation, it is possible to gradually begin to get the horse's longitudinal axis adapted to the circle. With a young horse this must be done particularly carefully so that he does not become afraid and try to fight against the side reins.

In the initial stages, the young horse should not be forced into a clear flexion of the head to the inside by means of shortening the inside side rein: his natural movement is to make fast turns with flexion to the outside. This is why the horse should only be asked to adapt his longitudinal axis to the circle very gradually and carefully. Accordingly, if tension is anticipated, the inside side rein should not be fastened shorter than the outside one at first, because this can give the horse a feeling of claustrophobia.

Only when the horse has become accustomed to the side reins and it is certain that he will not become afraid of them, can the inside side rein be shortened more than the outside one and the horse then flexed more to the inside. Under these conditions the horse can be suppled-up more quickly than when he is going straight or flexed to the outside.

On this subject the great classical dressage trainer Nuno Oliveira said very aptly: "The horse should always be a banana—he should never become a straight iron pole!" Keep in

"It is only when the horse is going straight that it is possible, with the right degree of collection, to engage the hindquarters more and, as a result of increased flexion, to achieve good suppleness. This helps the balance and smoothness as well as strengthening the hindquarters for more demanding exercises."
Alois Podhajsky

mind that frequent changes of rein improve elasticity and prevent tension. Gradually, by means of constantly extending and reducing the circle, with lots of changes of pace, more intensive work can be done on the horse's convex side, normally the right. However, this should not be overdone: setting the level of requirement very high does not necessarily achieve optimum success!

23 *Frequent changes in the size of the circle, the paces and gaits, and the stride length, will maintain the horse's attentiveness toward the trainer's demands.*

DRAW REINS

I recommend draw reins for a sensitive horse because he does not feel as restricted as with side reins and, if they are attached low, they can encourage the forward and downward stretching of the neck without causing the nose to come behind the vertical. Beware, however, that when they are attached lower, moving between the horse's legs, they stabilize the horse's neck less than rigid side reins do, thus necessitating very gentle contact on the longe line so that the horse's head is not pulled over the inside front leg. If this mistake

24 *The horse stepping sideways and ...*

cannot be eliminated, it is better not to use draw reins attached in a low position when longeing. However, even when they are attached on the side, thus stabilizing the horse's neck more, the horse normally finds them more pleasant than rigid side reins and they help the horse to relax more quickly.

CHANGE OF REIN

An effective way of preparing for a rein change is to stop the horse on the circle. If the horse does not stop from a walk when the command is given, the trainer should move quickly forward in the direction of the circle in order to block off the horse's path, and repeat the command. Praise the horse when he stops as a result of this intervention. In the course of this, quickly gather up the longe line in large, tidy loops and put the whip under the arm on the side that will hold the whip after the rein change has taken place.

If the exercise is carried out correctly, the horse will usually stop after just a few repetitions if the command is linked to small half-halts and the trainer moves slightly forward in the direction of the circle. It is not long before the trainer can get the horse to stop without moving from the center of the

circle. Then, collecting up the longe line and whip, the train- er should approach the horse from an angle so that he does not turn toward the trainer but rather waits on the circle to find out what is expected of him.

25 ...letting the horse move forward normally again on the circle line.

By means of a forehand or hindquarter turn, the horse then turns on the circle and, following the change of direc- tion, continues at a walk. The trainer stays far enough behind the horse not to restrict his forward impulsion, and brings him back into contact with the longe line. The whip should be pulled forward again immediately and not hidden behind the back.

If this procedure goes smoothly and without any difficul- ty, the horse can then be allowed to come into the middle of the circle to change the rein, and from there be sent back again on to the circle. However, unless the horse is well capa- ble of doing this, do not use this form of rein change too soon.

LATERAL STEPS

As soon as the trainer has moved on to longeing the horse alone, he can also begin letting him take some lateral steps. The starting point for this is a halt in the center of the circle.

When the horse moves on at a walk, hold a crop or longe whip horizontally at the height of the horse's stifle, driving him sideways. If he moves sideways away from the whip, after a few steps allow him to go forward on the circle (figs. 24 and 25).

Longeing an Advanced Horse

Longeing the young horse serves as preparation for work under the rider. Longeing an advanced horse can keep him in form and improve his elasticity without undue strain. Longeing prior to riding can be a help here: without the rider's weight, the horse relaxes more quickly and easily than with a rider on his back, and then, in a fresh state, he can move on to work under the rider, which naturally requires more of him.

CONTACT

With an advanced horse, pay careful attention to clean transitions, even on the longe line. You can best achieve this by means of a good connection between the hand and the cavesson. Unlike when longeing a horse that is being prepared for showing in hand—moving him on a loose longe line—when working with a dressage horse intended to be ridden under saddle, the longe should be just slightly taut.

Move the whiplash in the direction of the horse's shoulder until he enlarges the circle and establishes a sufficiently close contact. If this doesn't work, shake the longe line in such a way that it forms a kind of serpentine (fig. 26). This has a threatening effect on the horse and usually causes him to enlarge the circle. Increase the intensity of this movement and the desired contact occurs. If the necessary contact is then established, the trainer can introduce each command by simply closing and relaxing his hand again.

The trainer's state of mind is reflected in the influence of his hand. If he is relaxed and exuding an air of calm, this calmness is transferred to the horse. It is often enough for the trainer simply to act as though he is calm and in charge of the situation and this message alone will indeed calm both horse and trainer.

Remember that one should always try to achieve the desired effect with a minimum amount of influence. In addition to the aforementioned closing and relaxing of the hand, try to move your fingers without any alteration in the position of the hand.

If you want to make the horse attentive and achieve lively movements as a reaction, use half-halts—very short pulls on the rein with subsequent yielding. You can increase the horse's degree of attentiveness by applying staccato-style driving aids (clucking or whip cracks) in the yielding phase of the half-halts. In expectation of such driving aids, the horse will respect half-halts after very few repetitions, even without application of the driving aids.

A fine horse can be so well tuned to halts and half-halts that a command becomes superfluous. It is always astonishing for spectators who are not aware of this connection when my father, Kurt Hinrichs, who is now 87 years old (and to whom, of all my instructors of in-hand work, I owe the most) asks

26 Shaking the longe line in a way that creates serpentine-like loops, encourages the horse to move away and reestablish contact.

27 *A horse that can be relaxed on the longe can also be brought into a lengthened frame quite easily under the rider, the beginning of which can be seen here with the 4-year-old Kladruber stallion, Generalissimus XXXI-2. A prerequisite is that the horse trustingly accepts an even contact on the rein.*

28 *Ureo, under Ruth Giffels, trotting in a long-and-low frame; the horse stretches trustingly forward and downward in response to an open hand.*

the spectators to determine the precise spot where a horse going at an attentive walk should canter. His horses actually canter in response to a closing of his hand that—even through gloves—is not detectable to the naked eye! This effect can, however, only succeed if the horse's level of interest is always kept up and he is not allowed simply to go round and round.

VARIETY AS AN AID TO MOTIVATION

The horse's level of interest can be increased just by constantly varying the size of the circle. The smaller the circle, the greater the trainer's driving effect is as a result of his position. Therefore, on a reduced circle, he only has to use the whip very sparingly in order to make his horse attentive, while on a

Important Aspects of Longeing

- The trainer should move confidently, normally remain in the one place, and give clear voice aids.
- The longe whip should lie comfortably in the hand and be long enough to touch the horse.
- The trainer should establish contact via his hand and longe line.
- Apply the aids in the following sequence: voice, hand, then whip.
- Use variety, and adapt your longeing to suit the horse's age and stage of training.

larger circle more intensive use is normally required. Frequent pace and tempo changes also help the horse to be more attentive.

Another option for increasing attentiveness toward the trainer is the use of cavaletti over which the horse can be longed, or longed past. Depending on the instructions given, the horse can be either relaxed or collected in this way.

All these variation possibilities are helpful not only for the young horse, but also for the more advanced, older horse, with a view to training that is as kind, gentle, and wear-and-tear-free as possible. It is very good, even for an experienced and well-trained horse, to be relaxed again on the longe line without the rider's weight and to experience some variety in the training schedule as a result of constructive longeing.

In addition to longeing, work in hand on a short rein without the rider's weight, offers further opportunities for varied preparation of the horse for the work under the rider. With work in hand, you can more clearly differentiate between the aids and their effect than you can by longeing, and other exercises, which can not be done on the longe line at all (or certainly not done with great precision), can be carried out.

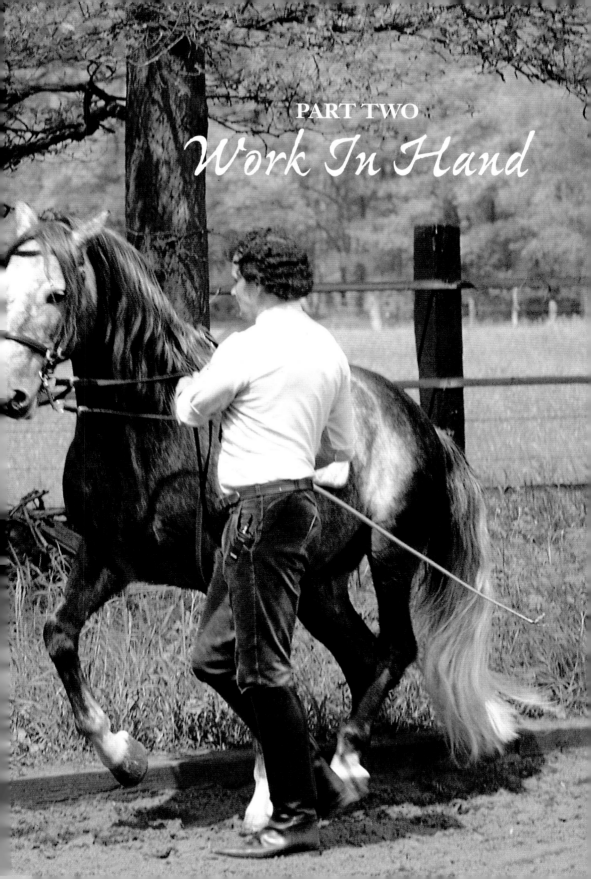

PART TWO

Work In Hand

Equipment and Aids

29 *The Lipizzaner stallion, Pluto Roviga: working on the levade.*

The items of equipment you will need for work in hand have, for the most part, already been mentioned in the section on longeing. A leading rein is one extra item that is helpful because it is easier to handle than the long longe line.

Which whip is used for in-hand work depends on which particular lesson is being worked on at the time, as well as the personality of the trainer and temperament of the horse. For lessons that involve lively action of the horse, like the piaffe, the whip has to be so elastic that it can be used to make a light vibration that can be transferred to the horse. A curved whip with which, moving on the inside, it is possible to touch both hind legs, is also suitable for this work (see fig. 30).

On the other hand, an inflexible whip is often more suitable for lessons when you want a calm reaction, such as the Spanish walk or the passage. An inflexible whip is also better for those who want to practice work in hand and who have difficulty with the precision of their own coordination when guiding the whip. Anyone who is not yet in a position to control a flexible whip with the necessary degree of precision should use a firm whip in order to avoid unnecessarily irritating the horse.

The length of the whip should correspond to the size of the horse and the intended lesson: one should always be in a position to touch the horse with the end of the whip. For a medium-sized horse, 60 inches (150–160 cm) is a good length for work in hand. Touching the horse with more than the tip of the whip should always remain an exception—and should only be done when the horse needs to gain trust and confidence in the whip. Whips that are used for driving a horse into the piaffe during work in hand combined with an independently active rider should be rather longer for safety reasons, but for certain exercises, such as raising the forelegs, a normal length riding whip of 42 inches (100–110 cm) is sufficient.

Whips for work in hand, just like longeing whips, should be light and comfortable to hold, so that the trainer feels at ease and is in no way hampered by equipment that is not entirely suitable for his work. Remember that if the whip is made of wood rather than plastic, it must be very carefully looked after and hung up after use or placed on a flat surface so that it does not become warped. If a natural wood crop is used, then pay attention to the fact that the property of the whip will change according to the varying moisture content!

With high moisture content, the whip moves better than it does with low moisture content. If natural whips, therefore, are to maintain their flexibility, then they should be placed in water after being cut off. If this is not done they will soon not bend anymore. The changing consistency of a natural whip can mean that the horse is more attentive to it than toward a synthetic whip of constant quality.

The color of the whip can be significant: a dark one is less noticeable than a light one. A highly strung, or nervous horse

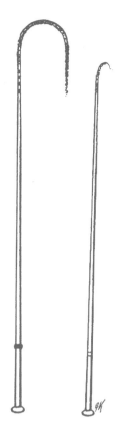

30 *A curved whip (left) can be helpful when touching both forelegs. A work-in-hand whip (right) facilitates a precise application.*

should not be subjected to the additional disturbance of a white whip. In such a case a black one would be preferable. On the other hand, an unmotivated horse can become more attentive solely through seeing a lighter-colored whip.

Anyone with serious appreciation of his whip as a valuable work tool does not simply throw it down on the ground while working with the horse. In addition to normal aspects of care, this behavior, which can be so often observed, also defies safety considerations—and, moreover, indicates a lack of good equestrian manners.

Champing the Bit In Hand

A lot of tension in the horse's mouth, poll, and neck area that becomes evident under the rider can be gently overcome through flexing exercises in hand. To do this, the trainer positions himself in front of the horse and straightens him, with a vertically positioned head. By means of light pulls on the reins, the head is slowly positioned to the left and then to the right. During this exercise it is important that the horse starts to champ on the bit. When this has been achieved, take a very gentle contact with a calm hand. The horse experiences this as a reward for lateral yielding and champing.

Not every horse starts to champ automatically as a reaction to the lateral flexing. But champing is a sign of the fact that the horse is relaxing, and only a relaxed horse respects subtle rein aids. The champing, therefore, is quite definitely required as an element of submissiveness for work under the rider.

With horses that do not start to champ of their own accord, it is possible to cause the horse to open his mouth and start champing during the bending. While still standing in front of the horse, pull the outside ring of the bit forward, so that side of the bit will press against the roof of the horse's mouth. At the same time, push the inside ring backward so that the side of the bit presses on the tongue and bar of the mouth (see fig. 31). When, for example, the horse's head is bent to his left, pull the left bit ring toward you, and push the right ring back toward the horse. When the horse opens his mouth, and starts champing, stop pulling the bit rings immediately and praise the horse so that he understands that the champing is what is expected. In this way, relaxed champing can be a learned process without stress.

If the horse does not champ after opening the mouth and instead simply closes the mouth again, don't worry. Just repeat the action of opening the mouth from a relaxed basic position. In most cases the horse will begin champing after just a few repetitions and, later on, this will work immediately when these bending exercises are done. If the horse continues not to champ, check to be certain the bridle is not too tight making it impossible for him to open his mouth.

31 Encouraging the horse to champ the bit.

Some horses that are particularly difficult to get to champ can be encouraged by giving a treat after getting them to open the mouth. Pieces of apple have proved particularly successful for me.

A horse that has learned to champ in hand will also keep up this behavior under the rider and thus react compliantly to actions of the hand—always, of course, under the condition that the rider uses his hand for the right purpose and does not confuse the horse by making mistakes.

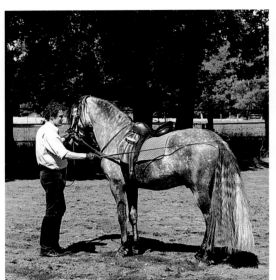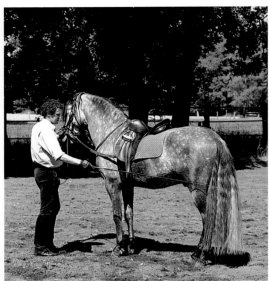

Familiarizing the Horse with the Whip

The horse should become familiarized with the whip at a very early stage. The whip can have a calming effect when passed slowly and smoothly over the horse's body, beginning on the croup and sliding right down to the fetlocks of the hind legs (figs. 32–35). If the young horse accepts this contact when standing still, then he should be praised warmly. In this way he learns that the whip is a training instrument. If the horse remains relaxed, the exercise may be repeated at a walk.

Work in hand can be introduced with this downward stroking of the horse with the whip while the horse is walking. This will help the trainer find out about the horse's general mood: since this type of whip movement generally has a calming effect, normally only very slight touches are needed to encourage the horse to step smartly forward. However, if the horse has become so calmed as a result of the whip that he almost stops of his own accord, try raising the whip quickly from the fetlocks upward. This has a stimulating effect and can be used as an aid to develop more impulsion and a higher stepping frequency.

 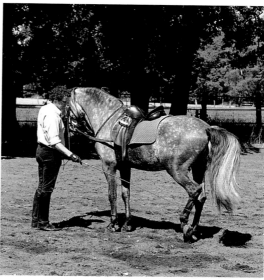

At this point I am quite deliberately not going into detail on the subject of touching the forelegs. This option should, generally speaking, not be used until a later stage of training, when the horse can be relaxed without any difficulty and, to a certain degree, collected. If he is not sufficiently prepared, touching the forelegs can provoke disobedience.

32–35 Getting the horse accustomed to the whip: a slow stroking from the croup to the fetlocks has a calming effect. From the horse's reaction to this, the trainer can draw conclusions about the horse's mental state and take these into consideration when applying the aids.

Lateral Steps In Hand

You've learned about teaching the horse to move out sideways from the longe whip or crop when going out to the circle. When the horse has become accustomed to this movement, lateral steps can be included in the training program as a relaxation exercise. Attach side reins to the snaffle and lead the horse in the cavesson for this exercise.

As in shoulder-in, position the horse's neck very slightly against the direction in which he is going, but not bent. Initially, half a long side of the arena (or less) is sufficient, then later on, this can be extended and the horse can be allowed to step laterally for a whole long side. When the horse is on the track you can better tell whether he is on the aids than you can if he is on a circle. The easiest way to make the demand being placed on the horse clear and understandable is to position the forehand to the outside against the boards or fence, which work as a visual boundary. Using the border this way means that, right from the beginning, only very slight rein aids are required. For a person without much experience with in-hand work, it is possible that at this stage the horse will take up too much of an angle to the side and may even do a forehand turn. This can be avoided by clearly focusing your gaze on the end of the side you are working on and moving straight toward it. If, instead of doing this, the trainer looks at the horse, then there is a danger that he will not go forward quickly enough himself, and this will have a definite braking effect on the horse. If the horse has understood what you want of him, then it is perfectly possible to let him step over with his forehand positioned into the arena without the aid of visual limits (fig. 36).

36 Doing some lateral steps, and then letting the horse move forward normally on the circle.

At the beginning the horse should always be positioned straightforward before he is stopped at the end of the exercise. Otherwise, instead of stopping immediately the horse

may turn around the trainer before he stops. To straighten up the horse, apply short, clear pressure against the head (in the mouth area) with the rein-leading hand, to bring him from the lateral movement on to the straight line. A horse should only be halted in a lateral position by a trainer who already

has sufficient experience with work in hand and who is in a position to prevent the horse from unintentionally turning around him or performing any other surprising movements. When such unintended moves can be prevented, halting at an angle to the side can have the advantage that the horse reacts more attentively to the trainer's wishes and can be better controlled, particularly as concerns the frequency of steps.

37 *Lateral steps. The boards on the ground around the riding arena form a slight visual boundary. High boarding, or a fence, would further restrict the horse's forward impulsion.*

Once again, it is important to remember that the trainer's demands must always be introduced with the voice so that other aids can be reduced to a minimum. When the trainer proceeds according to this principle, his intention is clear and his body language conveys appropriate messages to the horse.

BODY LANGUAGE

The trainer has to establish and maintain a certain authoritative space between the horse and himself in order to demonstrate his higher rank. Think about young stallions in a natural herd situation. In the case of discrepancies about rank, the lower-ranking stallion moves toward the higher-ranking stallion using submissive body language to indicate submission. The human being is always inferior to the horse in terms of body weight and therefore has to avoid disputes arising in the first place. In order to establish an authoritative distance to the horse, vibrate the rein. Vibrating hands are uncanny for a

38 The horse is kept at a distance with the arm quite stretched and the hand at the height of the horse's mouth. If the horse challenges this space, this distance can be reinforced by vibrating the rein with increasing energy, and touching the horse's head. The trainer moves along with the horse in the area of the horse's shoulder, keeping behind the horse's eye so that the trainer's body does not represent a visual barrier for the horse. The trainer should only move in front of the horse's eye if the horse tends to rush forward and a braking effect is specifically required.

horse so this effect can be used to ensure that the higher-ranking position of the human being remains beyond question (fig. 38). The trainer can even reinforce his position more aggressively by touching the horse briefly and energetically on the side of the head with a vibrating fist.

The horse should not be touched by the hand that holds the whip. Rather the whip is used to keep the horse at a distance. This task can be made easier by always keeping the tip of the whip nearer to the horse. This is difficult for anyone who doesn't have the relevant experience! In this way, by touching the horse with the tip of the whip, it is always possible to reestablish the proper space whenever it is in danger of diminishing.

It is also important that the whip is held with a sense of command. It should be held in such a way that—if the trainer were not wearing gloves—the shine of the fingernails could be seen from above. If the trainer wishes to reduce the horse's forward impulsion, and for example, do a full halt, he should, under no circumstances, move the hand holding the whip in the direction of the horse's hindquarters. This would unintentionally have a strong driving effect and the consequence of this would be to disturb the harmony.

For the inexperienced trainer it can be difficult to keep the whip constantly in a horizontal position at the height of the horse's knee to do the lateral stepping-over movement. Think of the tip of the whip as being a natural extension of the index finger. Anyone who has difficulties in doing this should always ensure that someone is available to correct him.

A fine differentiation in the height of the whip is necessary at this point if at a later stage you want to do lessons with the horse in hand without having him move out sideways. It is possible to drive the horse with the whip on the croup without having him step over laterally, so that he develops more forward impulsion. By way of contrast, in response to driving at the height of the hocks and lower, the horse shortens his movement and becomes more collected.

The trainer must keep his gaze in the direction of movement. If he makes the mistake of only concentrating on the hind legs, his body language is not expressing enough forward impulsion, but is driving the horse sideways instead (fig. 41). This means the trainer risks too great a lateral angle of the horse, as a result of which the harmony of the flow of movement will be disturbed. This mistake often also means that the horse departs from the line along which he should move. Once this happens, the trainer finds himself in a reactive rather than proactive position. Try to avoid this. The horse has to be reactive to the action of trainer and not vice versa!

Incidentally, it can be helpful to observe the horse's expression for short moments from time to time without, of course, forgetting to look forward. An experienced observer can see from the horse's facial expression how he is going to react and, by means of an action which the horse is not expecting, can prevent some fault occurring before it actually happens.

Anyone who aims to have a cooperative horse has to ensure that the horse has a cooperative facial expression. Once this has been achieved the trainer is well on the way to success! If, for example, for a period of several seconds or longer during the lateral side-stepping, the horse has both ears pointing forward he cannot be expected to react attentively to subtle halts. In such a situation the horse's attention should be

"Every rider has to be a psychologist in order to form clear judgment about the horse's behavior based on even the most subtle of indications—and then to draw the consequences from this."
Alois Podhajsky

Important Things to Remember During Work In Hand

•   Equipment should be suitable for the purpose and suited to the trainer's level of experience. In the case of an inexperienced trainer, I recommend side reins and a cavesson.
•   Establish space between you and the horse, and monitor it closely.
•   Turn the direction of your gaze away from the horse's body and toward your destination. Stick to your planned movements exactly. Don't just arrive anywhere. Avoid a fixed gaze in the direction of the horse's hind legs.
•   The tip of the whip points toward the horse, and the hand holding the whip must not touch the horse. Pay attention to a commanding and natural way of holding the whip, and convey a sense of confidence.
•   Keep training sessions short. When work has been successful, praise the horse and conclude the exercise.
•   The trainer's even stride length prescribes what is desired of the horse.
•   The desired action is communicated to the horse by voice and body language (the trainer says "on" and moves on himself, taking the horse with him).
•   Keep the lesson goal in mind and review it. Give calm but firm corrections, giving a positive instruction in the case of undesirable behavior.

drawn back to the trainer. For this purpose, speak to the horse shortly and clearly—in some circumstances also use a few tongue clucks—and if the facial expression of the horse does not give any indication of his attention to the trainer, use a touch with the whip.

If the horse responds by turning his attention to the trainer, interrupt work immediately and praise the horse. Then continue work requiring this level of attention from the horse and use a finer application of the aids.

In this way the horse learns that even subtle expressions by the trainer are to be observed and "politeness" is not an indication of weakness. If the trainer proceeds according to this principle, he avoids the risk of the horse testing out the limits of his strength.

The trainer must determine the direction of movement. He must exude a sense of authority and refrain from assuming a defensive posture. Otherwise there is a danger that the horse will sense weakness on the part of the trainer and attempt to take over leadership. Even a subtle sign of tension such as pulling in the stomach can cause the trainer to lose his confident vertical body posture and move the top part of his body

39 *(Left) Lateral steps. The hand positioned high in the picture has a stronger braking affect than a hand that is held lower. The height of the hand should always be adapted to suit the intended stride length. If upward half-halts are required, then the hand should be held at the level of the horse's mouth when the horse is doing lateral steps at a walk.*

40 *(Above) Lateral steps. Suitable auxiliary reins, and just slight contact, ensure that the horse remains almost straight in the exercise.*

41 (Right) A frequent beginner's mistake: if you only look at the action of the horse's hind feet, you will not notice until it is too late that the horse has taken up too much of a sideways position and is beginning to turn around you. When this happens, many people try to bring their horses back on to the right line by pushing with their bodies. This disturbs the harmony.

42 (Bottom) This is incorrect: defensive pulling-in of the stomach in connection with a slight forward tendency of the upper part of the body means that the trainer relinquishes the necessary distance from the horse. This mistake frequently causes dominance problems to ensue within a very short period.

43 (Right page) Lateral steps. The horse is quite clearly being kept at a distance. The whip is carried in such a way that the tip of the whip is closer to the horse than the hand carrying it. In this picture the trainer is observing the horse's expression from which he can draw conclusions concerning the horse's imminent behavior.

more toward the horse than he is actually aware of himself (fig. 42). This can give the horse the unpleasant feeling of being overwhelmed. The horse's normal, natural aggression will mean that he pushes with his body mass against the trainer in order to change the situation. The trainer can keep the appropriate space between himself and the horse by extending his arms (fig. 43).

In order not to appear cramped, it is important to convey the impression of feeling at ease in the very first attempts at the unusual body posture of work in hand. This means exuding a certain authority, which the horse experiences as being pleasant. The horse only trusts a self-confident, authoritative person who has no difficulties in how he uses his body.

> *The horse can only trust a self-confident, authoritative person who has no difficulties in using his own body.*

MANNER OF HOLDING THE REINS

I have mentioned that first experiences with lateral stepping-over are most helpful when done with a horse wearing side reins attached to the snaffle bit, while leading the horse on a rein attached to the cavesson. Having the horse's head guided by side reins facilitates the work for the inexperienced trainer: the horse cannot bend his neck so easily and go out of line via his outside shoulder.

There are, however, sensitive horses that react aggressively or nervously to the use of side reins. If the trainer is sufficiently capable, it is possible to deviate from the rule and work without these auxiliary reins.

When working with such a horse, the inside rein should be held so that the trainer can put his index finger into the snaffle ring (fig. 44). In this way, he can precisely define the position of the head. Initially, he has to have an image in his mind of the frame and head position with which the horse can best do the exercise in question. The image has to be adapted to the horse. If the horse has his head too high, a tug on the rein can make him lower his poll and bring the nose on to the vertical. The pull on the rein must be stopped immediately as the horse takes up the desired head position. At this moment, maintain only very gentle contact, almost the weight of the reins.

If, however, the horse pushes his head downward, it is possible to position it higher up by means of a short, clear

44 *Positioning the horse's head with the inside hand in the snaffle ring.*

45 *A longer inside rein makes it possible for the trainer to move farther back and thus for his body position to have less of a braking effect on the horse than when the horse is being led on the snaffle ring. The disadvantage is that it makes exact positioning of the horse's head considerably more difficult, and for this reason it is not recommended for beginners.*

pull on the rein, then to minimize the contact to an amount that is more pleasant. In this preparatory phase, it is important that the position of the horse's head is defined precisely to the inch and nothing is left to chance.

Allow the outside rein to slide over the neck near the withers. Hold this rein in the hand with the crop (see photo, p. 43). At first, it can be difficult for the beginner to find the optimum rein length. It should be long enough not to restrict the use of the crop. If the outside rein is too short at the beginning, let it slide through your hand, then close the hand again when a hand-height has been reached that makes it possible to use the crop with a sense of authority.

If the outside rein is too long, and the hand holding the crop thus comes into an un-

pleasantly low position, the trainer can open his hand, keeping it in contact with the rein, slide it upward and close it again at a reasonable height.

By pulling on the outside rein, you can prevent too strong a flex to the inside. To do this, try to manage it by firmly closing the hand and then opening it again without changing its position. If, under exceptional circumstances, this is not sufficient, then the outside rein can be taken away from the horse's neck and more rein length brought to the inside so that the outside rein is shortened.

I must emphasize once again that under no circumstances is the outside hand to move backward on the horse because it will have a driving effect and the horse will become unintentionally extended on the hand—a development that normally results in the harmony being disturbed!

THE DOUBLE BRIDLE

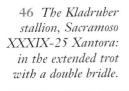

46 The Kladruber stallion, Sacramoso XXXIX-25 Xantora: in the extended trot with a double bridle.

Advanced horses can also wear a curb bit when working in hand. For this work, I recommend a double bridle using the Fillis method of holding the reins. The Fillis method is named after its famous user, British riding master, James Fil-

lis. With this method, the snaffle rein is guided from top to bottom through the hand, and the curb-bit rein in the opposite direction from bottom to top. In order to be able to change the length of the reins with clearer differentiation, the curb-bit rein can be alternatively guided from below through the hand in such a way that it comes through again between the index and the middle finger. Which of these variations is used is a matter of personal choice for the trainer.

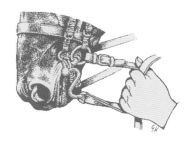

Using the Fillis method, it is possible to allow the snaffle rein alone to be applied. This is done by turning the back of the hand to the top and thus absorbing any pull from the curb-bit rein. Alternatively, it is possible to let the curb bit work more by rotating the hand so that the fingers turn up and thus completely exclude the snaffle. With the snaffle, the horse can be straightened, and with the curb, the head can be lowered and the nose brought on to the vertical. Thus, very subtle differences can be achieved with this method of handling the reins.

47 *The Fillis method of holding the reins.*

48 *The Kladruber stallion, Favory Ravella: being accustomed to the double bridle, and the Fillis method of rein handling.*

A certain amount of experience and ability is a prerequisite for using this system of working in hand with a double bridle. A trainer should spend plenty of time practicing his in hand skills before moving to a double bridle and the Fillis method. Once you feel you are proficient working with the snaffle bridle alone, try a double bridle but never begin with one. It's also recommended to work with an experienced horse during your first sessions with the double bridle.

Collecting Exercises

Let us return again to the subject of training the horse. The aim of the exercises described so far is to relax the horse. When the horse is sufficiently relaxed, work on the collecting exercises may begin.

An essential feature of collection is that the horse's hind legs come closer to the forelegs, so that more weight is distributed to the hindquarters. Once a level of collection is achieved with work in hand, collected movements under a rider can be directed by finer application of the aids. The horse that reacts to the slightest of aids will also reward the rider by taking more ground-covering strides. Determining the horse's ability to collect in hand is also useful for making decisions about the movements the horse is capable of under the rider without applying any undue strength. I will explore this subject in more detail in upcoming chapters.

Shoulder-In

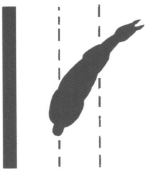

49 *Shoulder-in*

With the lateral steps so far, the horse was intended, in as far as possible, to stay straight in the hindquarters and only to be slightly flexed to the inside in the head and neck area. In the shoulder-in, he is to be evenly flexed slightly toward the inside from the head to tail. The trainer has to define the lateral position exactly. In dressage tests, the shoulder-in has to be performed on three hoof tracks, without any lateral crossing of the hind legs. It can also be done in keeping with the teaching of its inventor, François Robichon de la Guérinière, on four hoof tracks, with lateral crossing of the forelegs—the Baroque style. In this form, the exercise has a relaxing as well as a collecting function, and also makes the horse more versatile in the use of his legs. The horse then reacts better to subtle aids from the rider.

It does not make sense to over-emphasize the different philosophical teachings concerning the lateral degree of shoulder-in and invest all one's energies into expressing a negative opinion of one theory over the other. The important factor is that the amount of lateral flexion is defined exactly by the trainer, whether it is larger or smaller.

DEVELOPMENT OF THE SHOULDER-IN

The most effective way to relax the muscle system is with slow movements. With fast movements, there is a danger that the muscle system will contract again immediately after stretching. This is why the horse can be relaxed especially well in a slow-motion type of walk.

For the inexperienced trainer this slow, even walk may be difficult in the initial stages: for many horses this seemingly simple task is quite demanding. Such horses tend to press against the hand at an especially fast tempo and ignore half halts, or otherwise stop completely.

In order to avoid these two extremes, it is possible to allow the horse to take only one step after halting, then to halt again, and to repeat this request on a number of occasions. In this way, the horse is prevented from developing too much impulsion and applying it against the trainer.

50 *The shoulder-in on four tracks: according to the Baroque style.*

Not until the horse can be stopped after one step by means of a fine and subtle aid, should two slow steps and then stopping be required, and no more lengthy sequence of steps until later. If the halts are done on a horse that is not wearing side reins and is on a snaffle rein and/or curb rein, there is a danger that the horse's nose will come behind the vertical and he will shorten his neck. This can be avoided by giving the halt not as a rein-pull, but rather as an energetic closing of a previously relaxed hand. If the horse then contracts the neck, the next stage is to clearly pull the horse's head forward, using the inside rein and a softly yielding outside hand. The horse will subsequently be rewarded for yielding by means of relaxed, gentle hands and therefore learns how he should carry his head.

This positioning of the horse's head is, however, only possible when the horse's tempo—in the walk or trot—can be exactly defined. It is not sufficient if the horse that is initially nervous, does four or more steps in a rush and then lets himself be stopped in a fundamentally tense atmosphere. This is of no benefit whatsoever. Rather, the trainer must insist on being able to determine the speed of the first step and be able to stop the movement. Only if the trainer can exactly define the first step can the fourteenth step succeed in the same form.

In this context we should remind ourselves of the saying of the great Portuguese equestrian master, Nuno Oliveira, " If you lose the cadence, the horse begins to take command."

If the horse can already be commanded in his first steps, a basic attitude of rebellion can be avoided. The horse should be controlled in his movements in such a way that the trainer is not tempted to use force. Force creates disobedience. If the horse's disobedience is provoked, this can seriously endanger the continuation of trusting collaboration between

"If you lose the cadence, the horse begins to take command."
Nuno Oliveira

Important Aspects of the Shoulder-In

- Direct the shoulder-in by focusing your eyes on your destination and turning your body slightly inward.
- The leading arm should be extended and the trainer should have the head and neck of the horse clearly in view. The trainer should be positioned near the horse's shoulder, never in front of the horse's eye, which has a braking effect.
- Define the angle precisely. Too much angle makes it difficult for the horse to move forward and he tends to move into the center of the arena.
- When leading on both reins, frame in the outside shoulder with the outside rein. Do not exaggerate the flexion to the inside.

human being and horse. And without this, no high-class performance is possible.

Relaxing in slow-motion tempo, as described here, should, however, not be overdone or the horse may become bored. Variations at a walk, as well as walk-to-trot-to-walk transitions increase attentiveness and encourage elasticity.

For transitions, the trainer must pay careful heed to his body language. He himself should prescribe the slow-motion tempo with long, calm strides, and prescribe more lively movement with faster steps. If the horse respects the trainer's authority, he will adapt his movements to the trainer's movements. When the trainer self-confidently assumes a position of authority in such a way that the horse experiences this as pleasant, it becomes much easier for him to manage with slighter application of the aids than someone who is in constant doubt about himself and his ability.

The inexperienced trainer should always terminate the shoulder-in in such a way that he lets the horse stop in a straight position on the track. This avoids having the horse, after successful lateral steps, unintentionally turn around the trainer and have to be corrected. The trainer has to arrange the training structure in such a way that a positive working atmosphere is created and maintained. At the end of a successful exercise it is important to give praise and reward immediately in a rest phase. Do not correct unimportant, harmless mistakes at this point. Only a trainer who respects and regularly applies this seemingly simple principle of training that, sadly, is frequently forgotten, can motivate his horse toward a successful partnership.

The Shoulder-In and Its Relationship to Travers and Renvers

Before discussing the uses of travers (haunches-in) and renvers (haunches-out) in hand, let's review what they are. If the horse is on the right rein in the shoulder-in, then he crosses the forelegs from right to left. He is flexed to the right, and therefore, positioned against the direction of movement. In travers

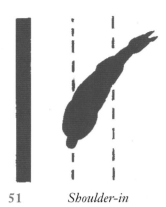

51   *Shoulder-in*

and renvers exercises, however, the horse is positioned and flexed in the direction of movement: in the travers on the right rein, the horse remains on the track with the forehand, the hindquarters go inward on the second track. The hind legs cross from left to right. The horse is positioned and flexed to the right—in other words in the direction of movement.

The renvers is a variation of the travers: the hindquarters remain on the track, and the forehand moves inward on to the second track. On the right rein, the forelegs cross from right to left. The horse is positioned and flexed to the left, which is also the direction of movement. Renvers on the right rein thus corresponds to the travers on the left rein, with the difference being that in the renvers the limiting effect of the track (and a fence or rail) is at the hindquarters, not the head.

With all travers-like exercises, including the renvers, work in hand should not be started until the preliminary exercises previously described (lateral stepping-over and shoulder-in) can be done easily, without any difficulties for the trainer or horse. This prerequisite should be fulfilled before starting to concentrate on the essential criteria of the travers lessons: the distinctive head position and flexion of the horse in the direction of movement.

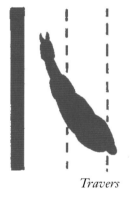

Travers

Development of the Renvers

First, stop the horse in the position of the shoulder-in (the hindquarters on the track, the forehand inward on the second track, the horse positioned and flexed to the inside away from the direction of movement). In a halted position, carefully change the horse's bend into the direction of movement as follows: for the renvers on the right rein, use the left rein to adjust the horse's head position. At the same time, support the horse's head with the right rein—holding the rein directly at the horse's mouth—to put the head slightly in the direction of movement, thus supporting the left position (fig. 52).

Renvers

This supporting of the head with the right rein can also be helpful later in the movement when it is a question of maintaining the flexed position. If the horse then speeds up too much in his movement, it is possible, as if squeezing out a sponge, to briefly and firmly close and relax the hands repeatedly until the horse's tempo and stride are corrected. During this process, do not move closer to the horse. Otherwise, as a result of the trainer's body language, the horse will be pushed on to the track and will abandon the lateral angle that is then difficult to restore without a disturbance in the harmony.

Any inexperienced trainer will have some initial difficulties here. However, it is important not to lose courage but rather to persevere and always to stop the horse when he comes out of his flexed position.

The trainer must remain calm and authoritative throughout. If he trundles along with small steps, then the horse cannot be expected to walk calmly with ground-covering strides. On the other hand, if the trainer strides forward with unreasonably long strides, the horse will not respond to halts by shortening the stride.

52 Renvers in hand: Christine Mehl with Girassol.

Important Aspects of the Renvers

- The introduction of renvers is from shoulder-in, where the horse is halted and his bend is changed toward the direction of movement.
- Forward movement is maintained by means of the trainer's fast and commanding walk. If necessary, drive on using the voice and/or whip.
- A frequent mistake is the loss of angle. The trainer must remain far enough to the inside of the track so he doesn't push the horse straight.

Important Aspects of the Travers

- Rein guiding is by means of both reins. The necessary flexion to the inside is achieved by taking up the inside rein.
- The trainer remains between the horse and the board or fence.
- The introduction of the travers is similar to leg yielding: the whip aid is used to put the horse's hindquarters on course—the horse proceeds on two tracks.
- A frequent mistake is positioning the horse at too much of an angle. Maintain fast, even, forward movement, do not drive too hard, and focus eyes on the direction of movement.

Whether the trainer begins to do the renvers exercises on the left or on the right rein depends on the direction in which the trainer and horse are happiest. Many people move better on the left rein, because the whip carried in the right hand is less difficult to hold. For this reason it is sometimes easier to start work with the side paces on the left rein. However, as many horses find left flexing and bending easier than right flexing and bending, it can be more pleasant for the horse if work on the renvers is commenced on the right rein. Particularly on the right rein, it is important for the trainer to keep looking in the direction of movement. Just keep taking short, quick looks at the horse's expression and under no circumstances fix your gaze on the horse's legs!

The renvers should be started at the beginning of the long side. At the end of this side, it should be changed to the shoulder-in or the horse should move straight on in a forward direction. Renvers through the corners is very hard work for the horse and requires considerable ability on the part of the trainer so that the horse does not disobey. In order to maintain the renvers through the corner, the trainer must be aware of the fact that the forehand must slow down and that the hindquarters of the horse moving in counter-position have to be moved around the forehand particularly carefully so that the horse does not feel trapped here.

Frequent changes from the shoulder-in to the renvers make the horse smooth and harmonious. It will also help the horse to accept the aids in lateral work under the weight of the rider more easily than if he had never experienced these exercises in hand.

53 *Renvers in hand: the horse's movement can be precisely defined.*

Development of the Half-Pass

To introduce the half-pass, walk on short side of the arena on the outside track while the horse walks beside you on the inner track. In the corner, move quickly forward because you have farther to go than the horse. After passing the first corner of the long side, position the horse sideways bent in the direction of movement on to the diagonal. Drive the horse with the whip held horizontally, at the height of the horse's knee.

Important Aspects of the Half-Pass

- The half-pass is a forward and sideways movement with a crossing over of the legs. The horse is bent and flexed in the direction of movement.
- The trainer is on the outside, as in the travers.
- The forehand goes slightly ahead, the hindquarters are driven from behind, with the whip held horizontally.
- The inner flexion is defined by the extent to which the inside rein is pulled.
- The hand holding the whip should never be pressed against the horse's body.
- Use minimal rein aids.
- A frequent mistake is half-passes that are made too steep. Look where you want to go and move forward all the time.

The exercise will only be a success if the trainer always looks toward the goal—on the short side, first the corner, from there a few steps to the end of the long side, then the end of the diagonal.

A common error is for the horse to move sideways too much and not forward enough. By increasingly using the inside rein without driving with the whip the horse can be prevented from moving away too much with the hindquarters, which is the cause of this problem. If this mistake has already occurred, it is possible to pull the horse forward with the outside rein to correct it.

If, however, the horse rushes forward too much, he can be corrected by means of a clear, short, firm closing of the hands from a relaxed hold, then relaxing again when the required stride length and tempo are achieved. Here, the trainer must remain relaxed if the horse is to relax also. A horse takes on the mood of the trainer. Therefore, it is important to make an effort to be as calm as possible. If, for some reason, you have to achieve an effect on the horse for a few moments by means of physical energy, it is important to consciously relax again afterward in order to continue exercising a positive influence on the working atmosphere.

If you have difficulties introducing half-passes as just described, you can also try beginning them from a half-circle. Coming out of the second corner of a long side—let's say coming from the left side—stop the horse parallel to the long side, following a half turn. If you expect the horse to stop incorrectly, position yourself in front of the horse to halt. Then flex the head to the right and complete the rest of the diagonal as a half-pass. This

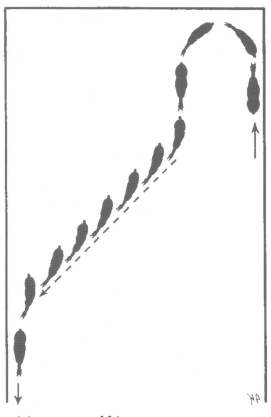

54 *The start of the half-pass out of a half circle.*

55 *A right half-pass at the walk: Ureo.*

*56 Trot half-pass to
the left: Girassol
ridden by
Ruth Giffels.*

introduction has the advantage that the trainer does not
have to move to the outside track before beginning (figs.
54 and 55).

To relax the horse, the first half-pass exercises should be
carried out at a very slow tempo without any great input of
physical power on the part of the trainer. It is a good idea,
however, as you do it more often, to change the tempo during the half-pass so that the horse remains attentive and does
not become bored. Transitions from walk-to-trot-to-walk can
also have a positive training effect.

HALF-PASSES UNDER SADDLE

Preliminary work in hand is a worthwhile investment to
prepare for half-passes under saddle. After such work, the
horse finds it easier to understand what is required of him and

is already elastic enough to respond fluently to the requirements. This means less work for the rider.

The horse's personal character can be particularly well expressed in ridden half-passes if, when training you practice the first part of the diagonal with a high degree of collection in the clearly defined lateral movement. Then, toward the end of the diagonal, increase the forward impulsion and reduce the lateral stepping-over slightly, in order to leave enough room available to achieve a clean conclusion.

If the horse is used to changing his bend in hand without any great strength having to be used, particularly by means of fluent transitions from one lateral movement into another, he will develop an elasticity that can also be used for zigzag half-passes under the rider. Zigzag half-passes are done between the long middle line to the centerline a number of times to the left and right, with the exercise terminating on the centerline. As a result of the frequent changes in flexing and bending within a short time, this exercise has both relaxing and collecting effects.

A horse takes on the mood of the trainer. Therefore, it is important to make an effort to be as calm as possible.

Development of the Pirouette

Pirouettes can also be prepared in hand at a walk without the rider's weight. It is easiest to begin with a half-pass, and to develop a pirouette from this in the center of the arena and subsequently continue the half-pass.

For the pirouette, the inside hind hoof of the horse is fixed by means of a fairly strong use of the inside rein. It can be released again if there is no strong likelihood of the horse going off into the half-pass again. If necessary, with a horse that does not know the exercise, repeat the clear aid on the inside rein several times during the pirouette. When the horse knows what is required of him, use of the reins can be gradually reduced.

Undesirable forward impulsion of the horse can be limited if the trainer is positioned well forward at the horse's head.

57 and 58 *Two
different moments
in a walk pirouette
to the right.*

The trainer should take into consideration the fact that he has to cover more ground than the horse in the pirouette. He thus has to move sufficiently fast while still ensuring that the turn is carried out calmly.

The initial, clear pull on the inside rein can mean that the inside hind hoof of the horse is so blocked that it is not raised at all from the ground. If this is the case, the inside rein should be loosened and the turn slightly enlarged as with the travers. Sometimes an appropriate comment from a neutral ob-

57 and 58 Two different moments in a walk pirouette to the right.

server can be helpful here. The trainer, of course, should only take a quick glance at the horse's hind feet because he needs to prescribe the goal of the movement by looking and focusing in the direction it is going if the exercise is to succeed.

If the pirouette is carried out in many small steps and the tempo is increased, tal-

ented horses quite frequently develop their first piaffe steps here. If this is the case, stop immediately and praise the horse! However, even if this result does not ensue, pirouettes in hand make the horse agile for work under saddle, and often make it easier to do movements at a canter.

59 *Canter pirouette: Maestoso Gratia.*

Important Aspects of the Pirouette

- The trainer goes on the horse's outside, has the longer distance to travel, and therefore has to move quickly.
- The inner hind leg of the horse has to be fixed; stepping away can be prevented by a pull on the inside rein.
- Use of a long enough whip will help to ensure the horse strikes off the inside hind leg.
- A frequent mistake is seen with the horse going forward too much. Use a visual brake by stepping in front of him, or turning him toward the rail.
- Another common error is a tendency to back up. So, allow the horse to take a stride forward from time to time.

60 *Maestoso Gratia in piaffe.*

Development of Piaffe

In a natural state, piaffe—a movement of diagonal hoof sequence almost, or completely, on one spot—can occasionally be observed when horses are excited. In this lesson, the horse steps increasingly under his center of gravity with his hind feet, which take up an increasing amount of his weight. This relieves the forehand and allows a higher action of the forelegs.

In dressage work, piaffe is not only a training goal. Even when perfection is still far away, it is an excellent means to exercise and loosen up the horse. The effect can be compared with knee-bending exercises for human beings. It is the task of the trainer to gradually develop this movement—even without the excitement connected with it when the horse does it naturally.

"RAISING" THE HIND LEGS

When the horse is confidently doing the work in hand described so far, he can be stopped on the track—initially on the left rein, if this is the easier direction in which to work. By means of slight contact with the end of the whip, approximately at the height of the hock joint or lower, he can be encouraged to raise the inside hind leg.

As soon as the horse reacts, he should be praised. Even kicking out should not be punished. This can gradually be prevented if the horse becomes used to raising the hind hoof from the ground in response to a voice aid (such as "left"), with the trainer only using the whip if the horse does not follow the voice command. Therefore, always use the most subtle aid possible first—here the voice—and only reinforce this with a more forceful aid if absolutely necessary. Sensitive horses that find the tickling sensation with the tip of the whip unpleasant will very quickly learn to avoid this by lifting the leg promptly.

In the case of less sensitive horses, the voice command can be followed by a short, light crack of the whip in order to make clear to the horse that the friendliness of the trainer is not to be understood as the same thing as weakness.

I must again emphasize a point I made earlier: if the trainer can always increase the intensity of the aids, and make the horse aware that he can do so, this will also increase his authority. (This does not only apply when dealing with horses!)

61 *Raising a hind leg.*

If the trainer has always left room to increase the intensity of the aids, and makes sure the horse is aware of this fact, the trainer's authority will increase.

When the horse's reaction corresponds to the trainer's expectations, the aids should be minimized immediately.

Next, the horse can be asked, in the same way, to raise the outside (here, right) hind leg. Remember to use the voice aid ("right"). With a normally talented horse, the procedure is to start off at a walk and then let him take a few steps at a collected trot in order to prepare for piaffe.

After a few repetitions, it is possible to go almost directly into the collected trot from a halt. This encourages the horse's attentiveness. If preparation at a walk takes too long, attentiveness is lost and too much thrust and too little carrying power are developed at a trot. This makes the horse difficult for the trainer to handle.

If, however, the horse immediately goes into a collected trot, his full attentiveness can be used to get him to step off with his hind hoof in response to a command ("left" or "right"). Many correctly prepared horses relax in response to well-known commands. At the first attempt it can often be observed that horses try to stand still with the front legs in order to raise the hind legs, and thus reduce the space between the front and hind legs themselves. This tendency should initially be encouraged, even if it means the horse raises the hind feet too high and the front feet too little so that the diagonal hoof sequence cannot always be established.

This sort of start is particularly suitable for people who, as yet, are not particularly experienced in teaching piaffe. They lose their fear that the horse could run away from them in these piaffe attempts and thus develop the necessary self-confidence. When this has been achieved, they can reestablish the diagonal hoof sequence by letting the horse go into the collected trot and then halting him: a horse that already thinks of trotting in the collected gaits is more motivated than one that is forced to do work in place by means of constant restraining aids.

A horse with weak hindquarters can be strengthened by having him raise and hold up his hind feet. Encourage the horse with the voice and repeated touches on the hind leg to keep this leg in the air for as long as possible. Physical therapists have found that muscles are strengthened if they are under pressure for longer than nine seconds. If, therefore, it is possible to get the horse to clearly raise a hind foot for longer than nine seconds, the hindquarter muscles will be strengthened without subjecting the horse to other organic strain. It is possible, therefore, to strengthen and prepare the horse for piaffe by asking him to raise the hind legs repeatedly as described.

It must, however, be made clear to the trainer that by doing this, the horse gets used to raising the hind feet higher than is necessary for piaffe. In the case of a well executed piaffe the horse raises his hind hooves so that the tip of the hoof reaches a maximum height between the coronary band and pastern of the leg standing still. Any additional height is always an indication that the horse has not yet taken up much weight on the hindquarters.

62 Ureo: preparing piaffe from the collected trot.

63 *Bringing the hind legs in toward the forelegs...*

BRINGING THE HIND LEGS IN TOWARD THE FORELEGS

If the horse has learned to raise the hind feet alternately in response to subtle aids, then, as a further preliminary exercise for the piaffe, they can be brought closer together in response to a vocal command and a slight touching on the front hooves. Encourage the horse to stretch his head forward and downward, and to arch his back. The horse does not take up any more weight with the hindquarters—he pushes this weight on to the forehand. However, the back and hindquarter muscle system is stretched and strengthened as a result. The exercise is particularly suitable for horses with weak backs or weak hindquarters that, without sufficient preparation, develop a fear of collection.

The hind legs and the forelegs can be brought in so that a distance of only approximately 8 inches (20 cm) remains between them. In this work, the trainer must be content with very small progress. A good aid here, in my experience, is to slightly touch the leg from top to bottom over the hock. Any forward movement of the hind foot, however small, should be praised immediately.

64 ...and under the rider.

The horse should not be allowed to move forward, unless this is specifically required (described later). If the trainer wants to reward the horse with feed, then always do it with the horse in the low, stretching forward position. If this principle is observed, some horses will achieve the described body posture after a few days, but the majority only after some weeks or months. It will then have a beneficial physical and mental effect for piaffing, because the horse is sufficiently prepared for

65 This stallion's forelegs are not absolutely vertical when he is standing at rest. The front feet are somewhat farther under the horse than is normally the case. In this case it would not be appropriate to bring the horse's hind feet in closer to the front feet when he is standing still.

the new requirement and has no fear of being overstretched.

In order to start piaffing, the horse's head should be positioned higher, so that the forehand is relieved from strain and the horse takes up more weight with the hindquarters. I do not rec-

ommend the exercise for a horse that stands naturally at a slight slant with his forelegs (fig. 65). In this case, putting the front and hind legs together would, in fact, block the action of the forehand in the piaffe. If such a horse has learned to raise the hind legs in response to a slight touching, then a transition should take place into lively forward movement. If the forward impulsion is sufficiently firm, then you can ask for some collected steps.

Depending on how the horse behaves, there are a variety of different points on which the horse can be touched. If it is a question of driving the horse forward, it should be touched on the croup. If, however, he tends to rush off, he should be touched, after setting off at a walk, with short and energetic strokes from the croup to the fetlocks downward, touching, in particular, the hocks from above. When the horse then steps under the center of gravity with the hind feet, follows through and thus reduces the distance between the front and hind legs, the exercise should be immediately interrupted and the horse praised. This effect of shortening the distance between front and hind legs by urging with the whip should be done only once each schooling session. By praising him, the horse learns that he is doing what is required.

66 The trainer on foot supports the rider in piaffe by driving the horse on from behind.

Only when the horse brings his rear feet close to the front feet and has a well sunken croup can he be touched low down on the hind leg without risking his bringing up his hind feet too high and thus disturbing the diagonal hoof sequence. With this system an advanced horse can recognize what is being demanded from him just from the height of the whip: the higher he is touched, the more he should go forward, the lower he is touched, the more he should stay on the spot.

67 and 68 First piaffe from the young, Lusitano stallion, Imalaia, and then the releasing-forward movement at the trot.

PIAFFE DEVELOPMENT UNDER SADDLE

With some horses in piaffe it is easier to maintain the forward impulsion of movement under the rider. In expectation of the trot, the horse becomes more fluent in piaffe style steps as a freeing forward movement. This should not, however, be practiced over too long a period, or the horse will only piaffe when the trainer is on the ground driving from behind. This is why transitions from piaffe to trot under the rider should soon be practiced without help from below, even if they do not succeed perfectly.

TROT–REIN BACK–TROT TRANSITIONS

If the horse has learned to raise the forelegs individually as a result of slight touching, then transitions from trot to rein back to trot in hand can help to establish the diagonal hoof

69 *Christiane Horstmann with her Camargue stallion, Guapo, on the way to piaffe. Straightening the horse's spine is made easier when two people are available for the work in hand.*

sequence and submissiveness. Clear commands and the effect of body language make clear to the horse what is required of him.

In the transition from rein back to trot, some horses become so tense that the harmony in the collaboration between human being and horse is disturbed. It can be helpful to go into a walk first after the rein back, and then to proceed from a walk to a trot. If the horse already thinks about the rein back in the forward movement, and in the rein back thinks about the trot, it does not have much farther to go to the piaffe.

The goal is for the horse to become collected after a very short phase of moving on in short diagonal steps. It is important here that the trainer also shortens the length of his own steps. The horse then adapts to him.

Starting to piaffe is easier if a helper can lead the horse. The trainer can concentrate on driving on and can analyze the situation better from a greater distance. Here it is important that the trainer, who is driving the horse at the beginning of each exercise, makes clear to the helper at the horse's head

70 *The Friesian stallion, Fumagalli, in piaffe, ridden by Andrea Schmitz.*

how the next work phase should be. He should also give a clear sign for the beginning and end of the exercise. Voice aids should only come from him because he is in the position to reinforce them with the whip, if necessary.

If the helper who is leading the horse at the head is not able to keep the horse straight, the trainer can attach a longe to the outer cavesson or snaffle ring and let it run over the withers to the inside into his inner hand. In this way he can have an additional active effect on the horse that is not possible from the position of the horse's shoulder.

TRANSITIONS FROM SHOULDER-IN TO PIAFFE

A further method of developing piaffe is from the shoulder-in. Increase the horse's gait in the shoulder-in (at a walk) until he begins to move in a diagonal hoof sequence. The first two collected steps that a horse takes when it moves straight on from the shoulder-in at a walk are less demanding for the horse than a short trot in the shoulder-in.

Since the ground covered by the movement forward is restricted by the sideways stepping-over, do not add further restriction with your hand. After the first piaffe-type steps, the trainer should halt the horse immediately and praise him (fig. 71).

71 Nardo developing piaffe from the shoulder-in.

Anyone who does not get the horse to piaffe in accordance with this structure has possibly made the mistake of boring the horse with a shoulder-in phase that was too long. Only if the stepping frequency and the expression of the movement are increased at the same time in the shoulder-in, will the horse be so attentive that he goes

The optimum tempo to piaffe for many large horses is between 90 and 100 steps per minute. If you have difficulty getting a sense for the tempo, use a metronome.

into piaffe-style steps of his own accord without sharp driving on.

The horse must feel the energy of the trainer rather like a crescendo in music. The trainer has to pay attention to the fact that he only touches the horse with the vibrating tip of the whip if he wants to have an activating effect. Sharp driving on from the middle of the whip, by contrast, leads to a resistant horse that holds back and, in the worst case, disobeys, both of which are clearly counterproductive.

The trainer must also be able to visualize the horse in the optimum piaffe in his "mind's eye" and convey the conviction that he will achieve his goal. Even when the trainer gets an unsatisfactory result, this visualization should not fade.

ESTABLISHING CADENCE WITH THE VOICE

With some horses, voice aids can be used successfully to establish cadence, such as an even clicking of the tongue in piaffe. Here, however, the trainer, not the horse, must set the speed, because the horse's speed is usually either too slow or too fast.

The way the tongue-clicking is done can be varied according to the goal being pursued: with a horse that tends to step out too quickly, the tongue-clicking can have a calming effect if the click is pitched low and kept calm. If you cannot do calming tongue-clicking, use words that have the cadence you want, such as "tap-tap," always radiating as much calmness as possible.

In the case of a horse that goes too slowly, make your tongue-clicking more agitated, which makes the horse attentive because he is not able to predict which action will come next. However, an unmotivated horse can be calmed and dulled by even-sounding, tongue-clicking. If this is the case, just mark the beginning of the exercise with a short, staccato-like tongue click and, if the horse does not step on diligently, apply the whip shortly and sharply. Always be aware of the effect created by your tongue-clicking and, if necessary, adapt it accordingly.

As soon as the horse—even if not regularly—begins to move as required, end the exercise immediately and praise the horse. Then ask the horse to piaffe again, using minimized aids. A long break between efforts could have the effect of losing the alerting effect of the previous action.

The optimum tempo to piaffe for many large horses is between 90 and 100 steps per minute. If you have difficulty getting a sense for this use a metronome. The best method for setting the metronome is to make a video recording. Count the horse's steps, noting in what frequency the horse best expresses the exercise then set the metronome to match.

72 *A horse's brilliance is not seen at its best until he can work without the hindrance of unnecessary "aids."*

It is always surprising to find out what a difference there is in the horse's expression as a result of just a very slight change in the frequency of steps. Some people may soon feel irritated by the soulless clicking of the metronome. If so, it can be helpful to find music that is particularly suited in rhythm and tempo to the frequency of steps. Adapt the aids to the music.

Not only the rhythm but also the expression of the movement can be influenced by the voice. To increase expression, use a verbal command: "larger," or "more," pronounced em-

73 *The Hanoverian horse, Keno, 29 years old when this photograph was taken, is suppled-up in piaffe in hand, and prepared for greater demands under the rider.*

phatically make the horse move with larger strides. In this way it is also possible to make short-stepping horses take larger strides, for which they need more time, and as a natural consequence of which they become quieter.

The horse's charisma in the piaffe, or indeed in other areas, does not reach an optimum standard until the rhythmical influences of the trainer stop and the horse settles himself naturally into his optimum tempo. The trainer should never lose touch with this goal and should attempt to minimize the voice aids at an early a stage as possible. In dressage tests these are no longer permissible. Despite the great value of voice aids, equitation, and preparatory work in hand should not be acoustic events.

THE PIAFFE IN HAND WITH SUPPLING-UP FUNCTION

An advanced horse can be suppled-up, as well as collected, by piaffes in hand before riding. This option is particularly useful in the case of a horse that has to be worked gently and cannot cope with a long trotting period.

For this purpose, keep the first piaffe efforts in hand very short (a maximum of four steps) without too much attention to quality and with gentle driving on. It would not be right to expect top performance levels from a horse that is not yet warmed up. However, it is surprising how after a few transitions from a steady collected walk to the start of piaffe back to the collected walk, elasticity and tone of the muscle system increase. When correctly developed, the horse's movements become more expressive without application of any stronger driving aids. Finally, a horse will also offer a longer effort. Note that if you demand piaffe efforts with great expression that are too long, too early, you will provoke tension and disobedience in the horse.

A long-distance run prior to performance is not a suitable warmup for a ballet dancer or a boxer.

A horse that has been prepared in hand can be brought straight on to high performance under the rider. We have to remember that a dancer or a boxer will do gymnastics, but not a long-distance run in order to warm up and loosen up their muscles prior to a performance.

If you want your horse to maintain a high level of performance over a long period, arrange the structure of your training schedule in such a way that all requirements can be covered in 30 to 45 minutes. Consider the fact that horses of the Spanish Riding School in Vienna, which are worked according to this principle, normally reach their performance peak between 18 and 21 years of age.

Even if the horse is full of energy, working for long hours at a stretch is not physically possible. In the case of a young horse that is very fresh, the suppling-up phase should take a different form from that used with an older dressage horse that is already well schooled.

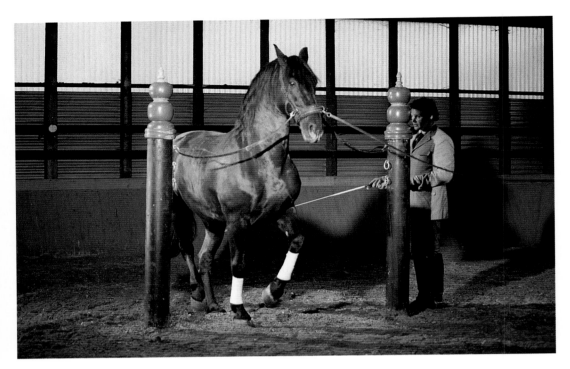

74 Maestoso Gratia doing piaffe in the pillars: the leading rein held by a helper (out of the photo) ensures the contact on the pillar reins.

WORK IN PILLARS

A further alternative for consolidating piaffe is working the horse in pillars. The pillars are two posts set into the ground at a distance of approximately five feet (160 cm), with rings at different heights to which the horse is attached at the side.

Even if there is no intention of attaching the horse in the pillars, they can be helpful as a form of "catalytic converter" in the arena. This particularly applies for horses that knock against the boarding with every step when they go into piaffe on the track and then tend to pay more attention to the crashing noise than to the trainer. It is indeed possible to eliminate this mistake by having a helper lead the horse while the trainer himself uses the whip on the outside of the croup to keep the hindquarters from falling out, and the hind feet coming under the body. It is helpful to move or work such a horse (while piaffing) around a pillar, if the trainer is alone. If pillars are not available, a tree or a similar object can be used instead.

In this exercise the trainer has farther to go in the turn and therefore has to go forward smartly although the horse is mov-

75 (Top right) Preparation to piaffe with yielded reins.

76 (Bottom right) Airs above the ground can also be done in the pillars: Maestoso Gratia in the pesade.

ing in the desired shortened steps. A lot of horses—even horses without any real talent for the piaffe—relax doing this exercise, in the course of which they have their eye on the trainer as well as on the pillar. With very few exceptions, the horses try not to touch the pillars when they are moving. In the case of horses with a higher natural tendency toward aggression, it is possible to observe how they throw themselves once or several times against the pillar and then, if it does not yield, they keep their distance from it.

The horse has to come forward and turn a little with every step. This combination also makes it possible for horses to piaffe that would not otherwise step forward with their hind feet on the straight line, but rather come forward with both hind legs almost simultaneously. These simultaneous (hopping) strides are particularly strenuous in the tight turn, and most horses that avoid piaffing in this way on the straight line manage the diagonal hoof sequence in the turn around the pillar. This particularly applies to modern sport horses with their immense propelling powers and resulting problems when asked to do very refined, extremely collected movements. Even the most untalented horses can learn to piaffe working in the pillars (or pillar)—providing the trainer manages to avoid any serious mistakes.

The horse should not be attached to the pillars until the first signs of being able to piaffe have become evident.

77 *Maestoso Gratia
in piaffe, on
yielded reins.*

77 *Maestoso Gratia
in piaffe, on
yielded reins.*

A very softly padded cavesson should be used for this work, or simply a halter if a cavesson is not available. Whether a horse should also wear a snaffle and side reins depends on how the necessary harmony can best be established: many horses feel less restricted in the pillars without side reins and therefore relax more easily.

Initially it is important for the horse to keep gentle contact on the pillar reins to avoid jumping into strong contact, which would cause pain. In the early stages, pillar work should be done with a helper holding an additional leading rein and standing at an angle in front of the horse. The helper must ensure that the horse takes up contact on the pillar reins (which should not be too long), and does not feel any fear. The helper should remain involved until the horse has become well accustomed to the pillar reins.

Lateral stepping-over at the beginning builds up the horse's confidence in the trainer's driving aids and motivates the horse for the piaffe. Correctly executed pillar work can in turn, be a good way to create an incentive for unmotivated horses, as well as to calm over keen, and restless horses.

If a horse has learned to piaffe in the pillar reins without the rider, then when a rider asks for piaffe on the spot he will not have to exercise a strong curbing influence with his hands.

A horse that has had this consolidating experience can also be encouraged to piaffe in other places, even with yielded reins. This is a good example of how beneficial work in hand can be as preparation for work under the rider.

The Polka and the Spanish Walk

If the horse's collection ability has been sufficiently consolidated by means of piaffe exercises, then the passage can be prepared with the help of the polka and Spanish walk. In the case of horses where the passage cannot be developed out of piaffe, it is possible, initially at a stand still, to encourage the horse to raise the forelegs in response to light touching (figs. 79 and 80). Touch the foreleg at the front with the tip of a firm whip. If it is a flexible whip, the horse will watch its movement with fascination without reacting to the touching.

78 The Spanish walk in the Royal Gardens in Hannover-Herren-hausen: Helga Syz with the Andalusian horse, Babieca; and Jutta Szentmiklossy von Primocz with the Lusitano stallion, Imbiri.

DEVELOPMENT OF THE POLKA

Exactly at what height on the leg the horse should be touched depends on the point at which the horse reacts best. This height should be used for the first exercises.

When the horse has understood that he should raise his leg in response to being touched with the whip, the height at which the whip is applied can be varied later on. It is possible to condition the horse in such a way that the whip applied between the coronet and the knee causes a round, circular movement, whereas the whip held at a higher level can cause the horse to stretch his forelegs. Even if the horse's reactions are minimal at first, the touching should not become stronger because it is important for the horse not to be frightened. Rather, the natural tendency to aggression should be used. The horse's attitude to a light touch with the whip is similar to his reaction to an insect that he wants to drive away.

If this exercise is repeated frequently and reinforced with praise and reward, the foreleg touched will be raised in an increasingly expressive way. The higher the horse's natural tendency to aggression, the faster the horse will make progress.

Once the horse has learned to stretch the forelegs out at a halt in response to light touching, then this can be started in motion. It is easy for an inexperienced trainer here to make the mistake of paying too much attention to the leg-stretching and too little to the forward impulsion. If you move backward with the horse during this exercise, you are even more exposed to this danger than someone who goes forward together with the horse in the horse's direction of movement.

Initially, the horse should always be asked to raise the same leg. Not until this works successfully in response to subtle aids should you ask for an increased action of the other foreleg. In the case of difficulties, a change of rein may be helpful in order to encourage the horse's willingness. Soon, the leg extension can start on every third step, so that the horse goes clearly forward between two lofty strides.

This exercise is called the polka. The command to raise the leg should be accompanied by a gentle rein pull and the use of the whip should be kept to a minimum, so that the whip will soon become completely superfluous.

It is easy for an inexperienced trainer to make the mistake of concentrating too much on the leg-stretching, and too little on the forward impulsion.

At the beginning, it is important for the horse to go smartly forward between the two lofty strides. When this is working well, be sure that during the stretching of the foreleg, the diagonal hind leg swings forward, thus maintaining the flow of movement. It is important to observe

that both hind legs do not remain firmly on the ground while a foreleg is raised. If this mistake in the polka cannot be eliminated, then the trainer should go back to the isolated stretching of one leg in motion. While doing this, the trainer himself should not remain standing during the stretching phase, but rather proceed forward at an even pace.

79 and 80 *Touching Ureo's left foreleg; and his eager reaction.*

Some horses tend to bend their necks and move at a sideways angle. If work is being done on a longing circle without high railings, then a helper can walk along outside the circle and straighten the horse by means of a leading rein attached on the outside. During turns, this helper has a longer distance to cover, and therefore has to move particularly quickly.

In the case of a horse that holds back, a helper driving gently forward with a whip on the hindquarters can also have a positive effect. If the trainer is completely alone, then he can use the whip, both to increase the horse's expression in the

81 The Camargue stallion, Guapo, doing the Spanish walk.

foreleg movement, and to move behind the horse's body in the direction of the hindquarters and apply the whip there if required. This makes the horse more attentive. Furthermore, the whip should only be shown to the horse's forehand immediately before asking for the more animated step, and then it should be withdrawn immediately, so as to not dull the horse to the whip.

Keep the horse straight during this exercise (fig. 82). If the horse is not positioned straight his head and neck will impose more strain on one foreleg than on the other. The foreleg that is exposed to the greatest strain will not be raised as high as the leg without the extra strain.

This knowledge can be used to your advantage when a horse that has experienced too much pleasure doing this exercise and, without any command being given, starts to paw his hooves while standing. Any punishment would only make the horse insecure and prevent him from moving expressively again in the next working phase. Therefore, instead of punishing undesired pawing or leg-stretching, and thus destroying the positive working atmosphere, press the horse's head over the foreleg that

he is moving. The increased strain blocks the foreleg movement. If the horse appears to be nervous and begins to raise the other foreleg, then press his head over this leg. Within a very short time, the horse will calm down and wait to discover what is to be demanded of him. Support this positive development with your voice.

Encourage desired behavior with your voice— "HA-A-A-LT," for example. Do not use negative commands, like "Stop that!" which will only make the horse insecure because he will not know how he should really behave. Encouraging com-

82 During leg-stretching exercises, it is important to ensure that the horse's head is positioned straight.

mands help to create a pleasant working atmosphere. The way that commands are expressed influences the body language of the trainer even if he is not aware of this.

In the leg-stretching exercises, verbal commands or tongue-clicking work well. Whichever form you use, it should always remain the same and should have a calming effect, while at the same time reflecting your conviction that you will enforce your commands. If the exercise is not progressing well, have someone observe and tell you if you are conveying this commanding impression.

If you are not yet able to express nuances (sometimes an arousing, demanding effect, sometimes more calming) with your tongue-clicking, stick to a verbal command and vary the tone of voice according to what is required.

When the horse willingly accepts the voice and whip aids, the rein aids become more significant: initially, you limit the leg-stretching by means of gentle rein pulling, then gradually the whip aids are replaced by the rein aids. In doing this, the trainer must convey calmness and the rein pulls should be given in such doses that the horse feels at ease with them. Half-halts should be avoided at all cost.

Gradually, encourage the horse to stretch the foreleg for as long as he feels the stronger rein pulling, then to lower the foreleg when the rein is released. Here, the side on which the rein is pulled is less significant than the moment at which it is done. It is usual, however, when riding the horse, to pull the rein more on the side of the leg that the horse should stretch. This should not lead to pulling the horse's head over to the side, however, because the foreleg movement would be restricted.

THE POLKA UNDER SADDLE

If the horse is prepared as described above, stretching the forelegs does not involve any real difficulties, even under the rider. At the beginning, the trainer should walk alongside the horse for support and lead the horse on the leading rein. The trainer always gives the commands, touches the forelegs—or merely shows the crop and takes it away again—the rider of-

The desired behavior should always be requested in a positive way. Negative commands will only make the horse unsure of himself—he will not know how he is really to behave.

fers support by means of rein, leg, and weight aids. The rider must ensure that he keeps sufficient contact to the horse's body with his legs. While the horse stretches a foreleg, the rider should drive the diagonal foreleg with his corresponding leg.

During this exercise, the upper part of the rider's body should be held well back and the horse should be driven on into confident contact on the rein. In these first attempts, many riders do not find their right position. Inexperienced riders then come slightly in front of the vertical with the upper parts of their bodies. This unsuitable transfer of weight—often not fully realized by the rider—is an additional disturbance to the flow of movement.

Many young horses tend to position themselves outward in their first attempts under the rider. Here, it is helpful for the trainer to walk alongside, using the leading rein to keep the horse straight. As soon as this can be done without further difficulty, the leading rein can be removed. The trainer can continue to minimize his support from an increasing distance, while the rider has to hold the horse's attentiveness with a competent application of the aids.

83 The Spanish walk.

84 *The 5-year-old Fumagalli: performing the Spanish walk with expressive action. Ridden by Andrea Schmitz.*

If the horse is overly keen and stretches his legs at every step instead of at every third step, then the rein contact should be somewhat released, or even completely yielded, and the horse driven forward more quickly.

A problem that frequently occurs, however, is a lack of forward impulsion. In order to continue creating the forward impulsion of the horse, the leg-stretching exercises should be interspersed with trotting phases, with plenty of impulsion.

Even if the horse gradually reacts to increasingly subtle aids, never dispense with the voice in the leg-stretching exercises. In this way, you avoid the chance of the horse stretching his legs of his own accord at a later stage (in a dressage test this would be extremely disturbing!)

In the initial period, many horses have one leg that they prefer to stretch and that they stretch more expressively than the other. In hand, as well as later under the rider, this can be remedied, in a kind of one-sided Spanish walk, by always asking the horse to raise the foreleg that is somewhat inferior. For example, assume the left foreleg is the one the horse stretches less enthusiastically. At a walk, ask that he always raise his left leg more when it comes away from the ground, while he goes forward with the right leg with normal walk expression.

If a horse, after understanding what is being required of him, suddenly refuses to raise a certain foreleg, then the Spanish walk, executed on one side only, can motivate the horse to cooperate more precisely.

If, for example, the horse refuses to stretch the right foreleg, the horse can be given the command to repeatedly stretch the left leg in a long exercise without a break, while the stretching of the right foreleg is no longer requested at all. At some stage, the horse will become tired of stretching the left foreleg and offers to stretch the right foreleg of his own accord. Halt immediately, and praise and reward him! In the next effort, the horse will also stretch this foreleg in accordance with the aids without any extra measures on the trainer's part.

85 (Left) Barbara Heilmeyer, with her Fjord mare, Thirza, at the Reken Festival is showing that an expressive Spanish walk is possible with a horse that is not a stallion of Iberian descent.

86 (Right) Maestoso Gratia doing the Spanish walk.

The Spanish Walk

After learning the polka as a preliminary exercise, we then come to the normal Spanish walk, where the horse raises both forelegs alternately in expressive style.

Initially, two steps are sufficient, developed from the slow walk, followed by the horse proceeding at a walk with normal expression. If a very calm flow of movement can be maintained and there is no disturbance in the rhythm, then ask for four steps. If the forward impulsion suffers as a result, then reestablish it with a transition to the trot.

The Spanish walk is best practiced in hand. It should not be done under the rider until it has been well consolidated in lengthy sequences. The Spanish walk is, in fact, not one of the classical school lessons in the strictest of senses. If the horse can do it, or at least the beginnings, it can be a good preparation for the passage if it is not possible to develop the passage from piaffe, or from the trot.

87 The Lusitano stallion, Fadista: in passage and ridden by Ruth Giffels.

Furthermore, the Spanish walk is an excellent means for getting tense horses to relax. If a horse under saddle begins to enjoy the lesson too much and starts to do the Spanish walk of his own accord, this tendency can be eliminated with a shoulder-in in a strong sideways position and higher stepping frequency, because the horse cannot continue to stretch his legs in this combination.

Development of the Passage

The passage is a lofty, trotting movement with minimal ground covered and a clearly extended moment of suspension. A particular feature of the exercise is the very strong collection: if the passage is executed in an ideal manner, the horse's forearms will be raised to an almost horizontal position, while the well-connected hind legs increasingly take up the weight and strike off powerfully forward and upward.

The expression of movement described here is dependent on conformation and talent. It cannot be expected from every horse. However, execution of the movement without any swaying sideways is to be expected from all horses eventually.

TRANSITIONS FROM PIAFFE TO PASSAGE

According to classical teaching, the passage is best developed from piaffe. This, however, can only be successful if the piaffe is done in a perfect way so that a transition to any form of the trot can always happen from it. If this condition is fulfilled with a large horse, it is only necessary to allow it to go forward approximately 2½ feet (80 cm) per step out of the piaffe, without changing the stepping frequency—and the passage comes about automatically.

Indeed, most large horses show the greatest expression in the passage when the tempo of 90 to 100 steps is taken over from the piaffe into the passage. If you use a metronome to establish the rhythm you will be surprised how different the expression in the movement is as a result of only a very slight change in tempo.

"The passage has completely different prerequisites from the piaffe. These attest to a horse a balancing ability similar to that of a dancer, who as a result of correct footwork, steps forward with nobility and elegance in his movement."

Kurt Albrecht, Director of the Spanish Riding School from 1974 to 1985

88 Two lessons with a good effect on each other: extended trot...

In the case of some horses that piaffe really well, it is possible to develop the passage either in hand or under the rider just by extending the ground covered.

What is important is that the trainer defines the exact moment and the precise step when the horse goes from the piaffe with a short stride, into the passage. The exercise can go wrong even in the case of a talented horse if the stride length in the piaffe is just extended gradually in the hope that at some point or other the horse will end up doing the passage.

The "piaffe forward" with long strides is not a suitable means by which to prepare the passage because it is difficult to make the horse understand that he should cease "sitting" on his haunches, and let himself "spring" forward instead.

TROT–TO–PASSAGE TRANSITIONS

A horse in true suspension in the passage can, generally speaking, only be achieved if the horse is allowed to go forward into the extended trot. This can be done better under the rider than in hand.

Horses that swing well at a trot can also be brought into the passage from the extended trot. This choice can be used partic-

89 ...and passage:
Ruth Giffels on Fadista.

ularly with many modern sport horses. In addition, by means of surprise transitions from the collected trot to the extended trot, and vice versa you can increase the horse's attentiveness toward the rider's aids. If the horse expects free forward movement, it is possible, with a gentle, firm hand, to get him to produce some expressive slower steps in the passage.

If you begin with the passage in this way, however, be careful to ensure that the horse does not start to use it as a means of defense and, when a collected trot is demanded and his hind legs are not taking up enough weight, he simply "swims away." In order to avoid this it is always better to start training piaffe before the passage.

TRANSITIONS FROM SPANISH WALK TO PASSAGE

In the case of horses that neither piaffe perfectly nor swing well at a trot, the passage can be gently prepared in hand if the horse at least understands the basic rudiments of the Spanish walk. The horse should have learned at a walk, when the command is given and in connection with being shown the whip, to raise the forelegs expressively from the ground, without causing the hoof sequence of the movement to suffer.

If that has been achieved, try a transition to a collected trot. In connection with the command to increase raising it, touch one foreleg lightly. If the horse then takes a step with even slightly higher action, interrupt the work immediately and praise the horse.

Just this one-off "raising" of the foreleg with greater expression is initially an increased demand on the horse. Usually the horse tries to avoid the increased strain on the hind legs by means of—perhaps even unexpectedly—lowering the head forward and downward, thus imposing more strain on the forehand and less on the hindquarters.

This unwanted reaction should be corrected as gently as possible with half-halts that use the rein aid in an upward motion, without causing the horse's motivation for further work to suffer in any way. In this phase, it is extremely important for the trainer to communicate clearly to the horse his satisfaction about the higher forehand action, while making the correction without any undue fuss.

If the horse gets the impression that the calmly held head is more important to the trainer than the higher foreleg action, then the trainer should not be surprised if the horse does not offer this action himself.

90 *How the check reins work.*

Some horses will not react initially to the aid for more expressive stepping action. In such cases do a transition from a trot to a walk, ask for a walk with higher leg action, then have the horse trot on again immediately—with praise of course! If the horse waits for the command to step more expressively, it will soon be possible to forego the transition to a walk. The trotting steps with higher leg action ensue almost automatically.

Minimize the aids for a more expressive step as soon as possible. Once this has been done successfully, ask the horse to do two such steps.

Sometimes it is necessary in the beginning for the driving impulse for the second step to be more intensive than for the first, which the horse is already expecting. Establish the horse's reaction to more subtle aids then apply the same principle to develop the third and fourth steps.

These expressive movements in longer exercises are strenuous for the horse. This is why some horses try to escape the necessary raising of the forehand by pushing their heads forward and downward. It can be useful, in addition to side reins to use a check rein, which keeps the horse raising his forehand and prevents disturbances in harmony. A prerequisite for this, however, is to get the horse gradually accustomed to this auxiliary rein while on the longe (fig. 90). If the horse is strengthened for the exercise with frequent repetitions and accepts the aids willingly, the check rein will soon become superfluous.

Do not be unduly disturbed when, initially, the horse only offers steps of varying degrees of expression, which are more or less stretched. The stretching of the forelegs can be converted into a rounder action if you touch the horse lower down with the whip at the front—around the coronets or just

91 Development of the passage from the Spanish walk: the driving aids are very low on the foreleg.

slightly higher—and in addition straighten the head more.

In the course of time many horses can be trained to do a rounded passage in response to being touched at the bottom of the foreleg and, by contrast, the stretched passage, otherwise known as the Spanish trot, in response to touching at breast height.

Both of these exercises, however, should only be carried out by someone who has considerable experience in the training of horses in the passage. If the trainer lacks appropriate experience there is the risk that the horse will mix the rounded and stretched form of the exercise at random and never achieve the desired precision.

92 and 93 Specific training makes it possible to achieve the desired rounded, foreleg action of the horse in the passage.

With many horses this passage with not-stretched, rounded forelegs will become an interesting challenge for the trainer to overcome.

FURTHER IMPROVEMENT OF THE PASSAGE UNDER SADDLE

After following the preparation just described, I recommend letting a helper sit on the horse. Initially this person should simply provide passive accompaniment to the trainer on foot, only gradually taking over more of the aids (fig. 93).

When it is no longer necessary to attach the horse to the leading rein, the trainer can increasingly concentrate on the driving aids: he can exercise favorable influence on the horse's action with a firm whip at the front and a flexible whip on the hindquarters.

Transitions from passage to extended trot encourage the horse's forward impulsion and make it possible for the trainer to retreat farther into the background. He should also ensure that the rider continues to minimize her influence in the passage. The aim is for the horse to respond to simple leg pressure and resisting hands, to go into the passage and remain in the exercise until he is asked to do another exercise. In the case of many horses, it is helpful to work with acoustic rhythmical influences in the initial period—similar to those used with the Spanish walk.

Some horses do not angle their forelegs enough and instead stretch them too much even after transitions from the passage to the extended trot and back to the passage. For these horses, turns in the passage, in particular serpentine loops, can help to create a rounder action. Be sure that the horse only turns, very carefully and gently at first, on every second step, when the inner foreleg is in the air as the free leg—or the movement will be lost.

The corners must be well rounded if the horse has the tendency to come out of the passage there. Halts on the outside rein should be replaced here by friendly, slightly upward halts on the inside rein, with firm contact maintained on the outside rein. Transitions from piaffe-to-passage-to-piaffe and lateral gaits in the passage can help to make the foreleg action rounder and encourage the horse to engage his hindquarters well, but lateral gaits in the passage are to be done at a very minimal sideways angle initially: the type of gait is more important than the lateral position.

Shoulder-in is the first lateral pace to practice. The sideways driving aid should be applied particularly carefully at the beginning during the crossing over of the forelegs in order to maintain the pace. If the shoulder-in is successful in the passage, then half-passes can also be done in this lesson over a

94 *Maestoso Gratia in the passage.*

lengthy period of time, again starting off with more forward movement and only a very slight sideways tendency.

There are trainers who disapprove of the type of passage development described here, but it can be followed by less experienced riders and horses who may never have a chance of doing it with other training methods. This applies particularly when, in the second part, after the relaxed learning of the slow, expressive steps, the necessary degree of collection is established via the activating of the hindquarters. Dividing the training in this way avoids unnecessarily stressful situations. Note that experienced riders with horses that learn piaffe and do passage readily do not need this type of lateral work in passage.

95 Girassol, in the passage: ridden by Ruth Giffels.

Long reining can also be a worthwhile complement and refinement to riding. Older horses that can no longer take much strain remain fit for longer as a result of collection exercises without the rider's weight. The personal relationship between the trainer and horse can be optimized through long reining: the trainer has no method of compelling the horse's response, and therefore has to make an active effort to motivate the horse for this voluntary work. A very fine level of sensitivity is required.

Long reining also provides an opportunity to observe the rein aids in isolation, without any modification by leg or weight aids. The aim of work in long reins is to be able to show all paces and airs of the high school in sequence.

PART THREE

Long Reining

Equipment for Auxiliary Aids

For long reining, I recommend the type of bridle used by the Spanish Riding School: the snaffle bridle. The reins should be long enough to enable the trainer to change sides behind the horse without any danger. Otherwise, it is not necessary to hold much material in the hands. As a general rule, I prefer that this work be done without either attaching side reins, or letting the reins run through the rings of a surcingle. This elimination of additional auxiliary aids places higher demands on the skills of the trainer but it also opens up greater possibilities concerning application of the rein aids.

96 *A suitable bridle for work in long reins.*

As far as the safety aspects are concerned, work in long reins should only be done with advanced, well-balanced horses that have well-trained collection ability. Horses that kick out at the whip are not suitable. The whip should be just flexible enough to permit precise application on the horse. The horse should never be provoked to kick—by being touched on the croup, for example.

Generally speaking, the trainer should walk with the horse so that he cannot be hit if the horse does kick out unexpectedly—either very close to the horse or at a sufficient distance.

Commencement of Work at the Walk

The horse should be made accustomed to the new task at a walk. A constant connection must be established between the hand and the horse's mouth. This may sound simple, but it is a demanding task for the inexperienced trainer. Anyone who follows his horse's movement intensely tends to bring his inside shoulder and thus the inner hand too far forward against the direction of movement. As a result the inside rein begins to hang instead of remaining taut, and the unintentional half-halts that ensue from the nodding movements of the horse's head frighten the horse and make him go behind the bit. All this can be avoided by driving the horse into a firm contact on the inside rein.

97 *Different ways to drive the horse in long reins: At considerable distance, so that the trainer cannot be kicked by the horse (top). Very close to the horse's hindquarters (below). (Note, I prefer to do this work without letting the reins run through the rings of the surcingle as shown here.)*

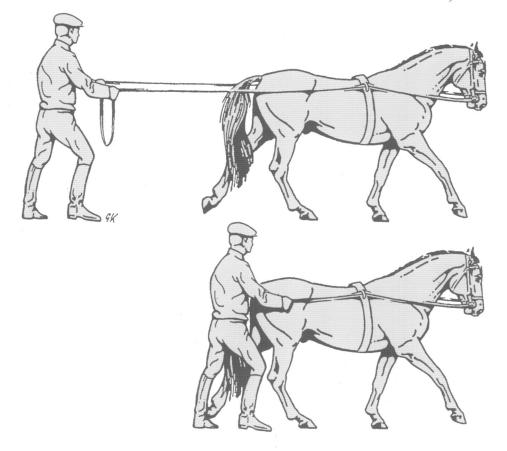

Changes of Direction

Turns should be introduced by means of body language. The trainer's eyes must be directed toward his goal so as to indicate the desired direction of movement to the horse. Even contact to the horse can only be maintained if, in the turns, the trainer moves his body in the horse's direction of movement. This introduces the horse's change of direction. If the trainer remains behind the direction of movement with the outside half of his body, this naturally means a disturbance in harmony. It is helpful for the trainer to always look at the goal of the direction of movement and to let his body follow the direction of his gaze. He follows the horse with even, long, calm strides near the hindquarters. As when riding, the hips should be held forward, the upper part of the body vertical.

In order to guarantee calm work with the reins, I recommend that the trainer place his hands on the horse at the beginning. Placing them on the hindquarters to the left and right of the spine works well. It may not be elegant, but it immediately gives an inexperienced trainer and his horse a feeling of security.

98 Work in long reins begins at the walk.

If a significant shortening of the reins becomes necessary, this should be done with calm, rounded movements. The hands must be relaxed in order to avoid the danger of unwillingly doing a halt while correcting the reins—this could lead to misunderstandings between trainer and horse.

If the trainer changes to the other side of the horse when the direction is changed, then this should not be allowed to interrupt the cadence. While changing sides, the trainer should not look at the ground because this would mean changing the position of the upper part of his body, which would subsequently lead to a disturbance in his feel for an even pace.

Changes of direction with the trainer moving to the other side should be practiced at a walk until these cause no difficulty whatsoever. If this is not mastered at a walk, it will not be possible to fulfill this task later without a disturbance in harmony in the trotting and cantering paces. Lateral steps in long reins can be done in all three paces. One should wait, however, until the horse has developed a certain forward impulsion at a trot before beginning to do these movements at a walk.

Transition to the Trot

Lengthy periods of walking are boring for a horse and tend to make him inattentive toward the aids applied by the trainer. Therefore trotting work should be started soon providing that the horse's collection ability has been so well schooled under the rider that the very collected trot does not cause any difficulties, even in long reins.

The trainer must keep up well with the horse and not just allow himself to be dragged along. In the first attempts, therefore, the trainer should quite consciously walk with his heel down first. This stabilizes the upright body posture. The stomach should not be held in as this makes it impossible for the trainer to determine the exact length of his strides and also has a negative influence on the precision of his hand aids.

It is only when the trainer walks along confidently with the horse that he can accurately determine the horse's tempo.

Aspects of Handling the Reins

A raised hand has more of an effect upward on the horse's lips and is more strongly respected than a hand positioned lower down, which is primarily felt on the horse's tongue and jawbones. Thus turns can be done more easily if the inside hand is held slightly higher than the outside one. The effect of this becomes particularly clear at a trot or canter when the horse has more impulsion.

Difficulties regularly occur in turns when the inside hand is held too low in comparison to the outside one: many horses then break away to the outside, the trainer no longer has proper control, and the turn becomes considerably larger than intended. This effect can also come about if the inside rein is taut in the turn and the outside rein is hanging loosely, thus hindering proper contact. The result is that the horse responds to unintentional half-halts caused by the loose rein.

Shoulder-In

In the lateral paces the rein can be applied so that it presses sideways. Shoulder-in is a fundamental lesson in long reins too. Before beginning, however, it is important to have found out whether the left or right direction is easier for the horse. In order to create a positive working atmosphere, it is essential to commence with the side that is more pleasant for the horse.

A horse that goes behind the bit at a walk and presents difficulties in establishing good, even contact should be driven on to the hand with plenty of impulsion at a trot. This pace should then also be used for the shoulder-in. The easiest way to do the exercise is with the hands positioned wide apart on the hindquarters.

At the beginning of the long side, bring the forehand inward on to the second track by means of a vibration on the inside rein. If the horse follows the aid, then by means of a half-halt on the outside rein, he should be prevented from leaving the track with his hindquarters and moving out into

Whether the first attempts are done at the walk or the trot, depend on the horse's character.

A horse that goes behind the bit at a walk and presents difficulties in establishing good, even contact should be driven on to the hand with plenty of impulsion at a trot. This pace should then also be used for the shoulder-in.

the arena. Slight pressure with the inside hand against the horse's hindquarters creates the sideways movement. Forward impulsion and sideways tendency can be maintained and reinforced with the whip.

99 It is essential to move with a commanding air, and long, calm paces when working a horse in the long reins.

Some horses tend to become exhausted in the sideways movement and lose their forward impulsion. With such horses hold the whip in the outside hand and touch the horse's outside hock from behind: the ground-covering, energetic forward movement of the outside hind hoof is very important for the flow of movement.

If the forward impulsion does not present any problems, but instead the horse's lateral angle is too small, then the whip should be held on the horse's inside—in the trainer's inside hand—and used to press gently sideways. If the desired effect cannot be achieved when the whip is held vertically, then it can be used horizontally for a short time (fig. 100).

The horse, however, should not be provoked to throw himself against the whip! If he does not respond enough to the sideways driving whip, then the trainer should revert to the preparatory exercises in hand for a short time. These should succeed in response to subtle aids before attempting to

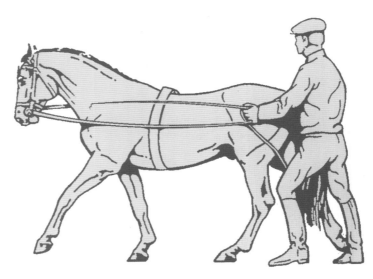

100 For short periods, the whip can also be used horizontally as a sideways driving aid.

do the shoulder-in in long reins again.

Over a lengthy period of time the shoulder-in should be concluded at the end of the long side without actively bringing the forehand back on to the first track. If you wait to end the shoulder-in until the precise moment when the forehand reaches the first track of the short side, you will not need an actively braking hand aid to straighten up, nor the associated increased driving aid.

In long reins it is as important as ever that fine harmony commences in the first training sessions if the horse is not to become dull. Otherwise, there is a risk that the horse will not react at all to the aids or, if they are applied more harshly, could even rebel.

COUNTER SHOULDER-IN

101 Counter shoulder-in

If you have difficulties with the shoulder-in as it is described here, try the counter shoulder-in as a simpler, preliminary form of the same exercise. Begin on the short side, changing your place at the horse's hindquarters to walking along on the horse's outer side. Before arriving at the long side, push the hindquarters slightly to the inside on to the second track while the forehand remains on the first track. In this exercise the trainer's attention can be more directed to the driving aids while the visual braking effect of the rail prevents the horse from rushing forward too much (fig. 101).

The Viennese Method of Handling the Reins

In the description of the shoulder-in I have so far assumed that the reins are being held firmly in each hand, positioned right and left of the hindquarters. There are, however, other ways for the experienced trainer to hold the reins. In this context I should particularly like to mention the usual way of handling the reins at the Spanish Riding School in Vienna, which has also been very successfully followed by the schools of riding art in Jerez de la Frontera, (Spain) and Lissabon-Queluz, (Portugal).

In this method, in all lessons apart from piaffe, passage and flying change, after a certain number of strides the trainer walks along with the horse with his hands positioned closely together in a riding position at the side of the hindquarters. This method looks very elegant and imposes high demands on the ability of the trainer (fig. 102).

The rein on the side on which the trainer is walking along runs in a straight line from the horse's mouth to the trainer's hand. The other rein

102 Holding the reins close together according to the Viennese method.

runs from the horse's mouth over the withers into the hand that is next to the horse. This rein—depending on the size of the horse—works more upward and thus more intensely on the horse's mouth than the other one, which does not cross over the withers.

In certain situations, for example travers lessons and pirouettes, the effect of the reins being held with one side higher can be very positive indeed, whereas in the shoulder-in, when the trainer moves along on the horse's inside, if the inner rein is not completely taut, the horse will get a "renvers tendency."

If, at the same time, the outside, higher rein is constantly too firm, many horses tend to position their inner ear too low. These aspects should be taken into account by anyone who would like to hold the long reins in the Viennese manner.

Travers Lessons

Before beginning with the travers lessons, the horse should be able to do the shoulder-in at a walk and trot in response to very slight aids. Once this is the case, it is possible to begin, either at a walk or a trot, with the travers on the track, which is also known as haunches-in. Begin on the short side with the trainer walking along on the outside at the horse's hindquarters, holding the reins according to the Viennese method. Shortly before reaching the long side, the trainer presses the hindquarters on to the second track with the hand next to the horse and at the same time collects the inside rein.

In doing this take care to ensure that this inside rein is held low enough in the hand—well below the horse's hip bone. In this position, by means of variable pressure, the reins can be used particularly effectively as a sideways driving aid if the horse has already learned to move away from the crop at knee level when working on short reins. Use half-halts on the outside rein to ensure that the horse's forelegs remain on the track.

Pay particular attention to an even head position and flexion of the horse in the direction of movement. The lateral stepping-over, following preparation in the form described above, does not normally pose problems so separate aids for this movement are not required. On the contrary, a common problem faced is an exaggerated lateral movement by the horse. If the horse himself moves out surprisingly quickly in a kind of forehand turn in response to the very slightest of sideways driving aids, and trainer and horse suddenly find themselves looking each other in the eye, the trainer should resume his place at the horse's hindquarters and introduce the travers with the reins held wide apart—in other words the hands positioned on the left and right sides of the hindquarters. This way it is easier to keep the horse in front and prevent him from turning around to the trainer.

A further difficulty can be keeping the horse going with his forelegs properly on the track and preventing him from moving away inward of his own accord. When preventing this, jerks on the inside rein must be avoided under all circumstances, as the horse would respond to these with a change of direction. The best way to avoid unwanted jerks is to keep a firmer contact. This should be maintained until both trainer and horse are experienced in long reins.

It is important to radiate a feeling of confidence, from the first attempts at difficult lessons in long reins onward. This includes controlled, deep breathing—the trainer should breathe quietly and evenly, in through the nose and out through the mouth. Avoid hectic movements in response to unexpected reactions by the horse, or he could become nervous and kick out at the trainer.

103 A half-pass to the right using the Viennese method of holding the reins.

Half-Passes

Once the travers can be done successfully on the track, then work can start on half-passes on a diagonal change of rein. With this movement, the same principle applies: direction before the lateral pace! If you lose sight of the direction of movement, you will not reach your goal. If in the half-pass, the reins are handled according to the Viennese manner—with the hands in a riding position and moving along with the horse on the outer side of the hindquarters—it is possible to use the inside hand, which is next to the horse, to push the horse sideways. The inside rein, which runs from the withers over the horse's back to the outer side of the hindquarters, reinforces this effect and ensures clear inner flexion (fig. 103). Once this has been established, the contact on this rein should be minimized, otherwise the horse will hold his inside ear higher than his outside ear.

104 Trot half-pass to the left in long reins. The trainer observes the horse's topline from which he can draw conclusions concerning the execution of the lesson.

In the first half-passes the horse does not move forward enough sometimes, but instead drifts off sideways rather more than is desired. This can be prevented by going farther behind the horse, if necessary also holding the reins far apart.

Once these initial difficulties have been overcome, counter changes of hand at a half-pass can be shown in long reins. When correctly done, as under the rider, they have a suppling-up and a collecting effect, as well as an excellent show effect.

105 Girassol: in piaffe in long reins.

Piaffe

106 *Possible arrangements of draw reins as leading reins: between the legs to encourage lowering of the head (top), or on the side (below).*

The piaffe is the next exercise to work on in long reins because it teaches the horse to collect, and a clear ability to collect is a prerequisite for cantering in long reins. It is best if the piaffe has already been developed as described—in hand and under the rider—before beginning to do it in long reins. There are, however, horses that learn to do piaffe more easily in long reins than in hand. Anyone who wants to try should always be careful to go with the horse in such a way that he can never be kicked.

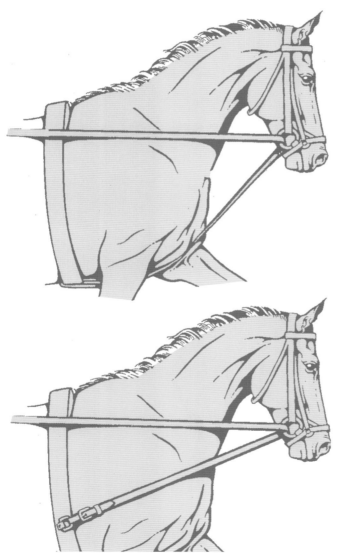

Piaffe-to-trot-to-piaffe transitions in long reins are a particularly useful training method because the ground covered by each movement can be infinitely regulated.

In piaffe itself it is important for the trainer to go with the horse in small, even steps to achieve regularity in the horse's movement. A lot of people have to consciously work for quite a long time on developing their feelings for taking small steps. There is a danger that the horse will make unintentional leaping-type movements if the trainer takes overlong strides, then stands still for a moment. On the other hand, he should avoid nervously toddling along with bent knees. This would reveal a lack of command of the situation to the

horse as well as to the spectators. It is, of course, also unfavorable if the trainer's movements appear to take more effort than those of the horse.

Many horses tend to become crooked during work in long reins, which means they then step unevenly. This can often be remedied by holding the reins wide apart, with the hands positioned on the left and right side of the hindquarters (fig. 107). If this is not enough to prevent an unintentional flexion to the outside, for an interim period it is possible to use the inner rein as a draw rein attached to the side of a surcingle. If the horse is used to having his head position determined exactly, the use of a draw rein will eventually become superfluous.

If the horse can do piaffe-to-trot-to-piaffe transitions in a relaxed and easy manner, then he should also be capable of doing a well-collected canter in long reins.

107 Holding the reins wide apart makes it possible to straighten the horse's spine in piaffe if he has started to lean over to one side.

Canter in Long Reins

Canter in long reins is much easier to manage if the horse has already been taught to set off at a canter in response to a verbal command, or a double clicking of the tongue in basic training on the longe. The precise moment of setting off must be exactly stipulated. The precision is increased if the horse is used to cantering on as a reaction to a half-halt on the longe, as well as under the rider.

108 Cantering in long reins: the trainer goes along on the horse's outside.

If the horse has been prepared in this way, he will canter on from the walk or the collected trot in response to the aids described, which should be applied at the same time. Do not expect more than a few strides at this pace at first. It is important for the trainer to move along quickly with the horse, and even after a minimal attempt at cantering, offer praise and reward!

Remember to gauge your praise to the response you want: a familiar word of praise like "g o o o o d" immediately stops the exercise and should be avoided. Instead, give praise in such a way as to keep the horse in the new pace as long as possible.

Do not apply extra pressure if the horse slips back into a trot after only a few strides in a collected canter. Instead the trainer should express his satisfaction that the horse has cantered at all, remain calm, and after a short break, ask the horse to canter on again.

In addition, it is particularly important for the trainer, even when moving along more quickly with the horse, to breathe in regularly through the nose and out through the mouth. In these first attempts it is best for the trainer to be on the horse's inside and to hold the reins wide apart. With this arrangement, the trainer has a shorter distance in the turns than the horse so that the horse's longer stride, which is still necessary, can be coped with more easily.

Choose the direction with which the horse feels most at ease at the canter. He should be able to do a calm, expressive school canter on the rein he finds easiest before making any attempt on the other rein.

Once the initial difficulties have been overcome and the horse canters well in both directions, you may try holding the reins according to the Viennese manner, with the trainer on the outside of the horse at the hindquarters (fig. 108). In this way, the flexion to the inside can be encouraged because the inside rein has a higher, sharper effect than the outside rein. A good, constant contact on this side prevents the horse from getting accidental half-halts, which he would follow by turning into the inside of the arena. If the horse, even with good contact on the inside rein, has the tendency to turn toward the inside, counteract this with half-halts on the outside rein.

109 *Canter half-pass in long reins.*

If the horse should position himself in a crooked, travers-like position on the straight line, he can be straightened up by touching the outside hind leg with the whip—moving downward on to the hock in connection with a taut inside rein—and some half-halts on the outside rein.

CANTER HALF-PASSES AND PIROUETTES

When holding the long reins according to the Viennese method, it is relatively easy to develop half-passes at a canter, because this method is favorable to the travers position of the horse. This also applies for pirouettes at a canter, which can be easily introduced from the half-pass with gentle rein aids to collect the forward impulsion, while simultaneously applying sideways driving aids on the horse's outer side.

It is best to give a command here that most horses can learn and react to within a very short time. The outer rein can be made to vibrate in such a way that the horse moves away from it in a sideways direction. With just the right amount of collection on the inside rein, the horse's inside hind hoof can be fixed without disturbing the hoof sequence of the canter strides.

Also in this exercise, the trainer should not lose sight of the goal of the direction of movement and, after the pirouette has been successfully introduced, he should indicate precisely, by increasing the forward drive (from far enough behind the horse), when the horse should continue the half-pass out of the pirouette.

FLYING CHANGE

"The flying change is cantering on out of the canter."
Nuno Oliveira

It is always best if a horse can do the flying change under the rider before doing it in long reins. It is possible, for example, to change out of the circle, and in connection with the trainer's change in position to the other side of the horse (the new outer side), to prepare the bending and flexion of the horse for the canter into which the horse should change. It is particularly valuable if the horse has been trained with precise and not exaggerated voice aids. One single tongue-click in connection with a slight, friendly half-halt can be enough to effect a flying change.

Particularly with regard to safety aspects, it is important to try to keep aids to a minimum here so that the horse remains calm and does not kick out as a result of excitement. Strong follow-up driving aids are particularly dangerous if the horse is behind the rein and the forehand is therefore under considerable strain, while the hindquarters are free.

Flying changes should not be attempted if the horse canters with lack of engagement of his hindquarters because then the smallest driving impulse can cause a horse to kick out. For this reason the trainer should always observe the horse's topline and, from it, draw important conclusions regarding the movement. If you watch the horse's legs instead, you risk disturbances in the flow of movement, which is very important, particularly with the flying change.

Whether, and how quickly, flying changes can be demanded from the horse in long reins after a particular number of canter strides, depends essentially on the quality of the preparation. If the horse canters on at the precise point in response to a slight, almost invisible half-halt on the outside rein in connection with a voice aid, and also does flying changes according to this principle, then on the long side it is possible to make the horse change toward the inside and then again toward the outside, initially with a change of position of the trainer at the horse's hindquarters.

When the horse has understood the task and is cooperating well, the changing aids—with the reins held far apart and hands positioned on the horse's hindquarters—can be applied without the trainer having to change his position.

110 *The canter pirouette in long reins: the trainer has to move along quickly so that impulsion is maintained.*

Remember the horse deserves praise and reward when he responds correctly! If he does not respond correctly then it is important to find out why.

Often a "travers tendency" in the canter, from which the change is supposed to take

111 *The Spanish walk in long reins: Christina Wolf with Girassol.*

place, prevents the horse from happily changing legs. If, however, the trainer presses the hindquarters just very slightly to the new inner side before the leg change, the voluntary co-operation on the part of the horse can be improved considerably.

Once the horse can change willingly and precisely in response to the aids to the inside and outside on the long side of the arena, without any change of position by the trainer, there is no longer far to go before the horse will be doing a series of flying changes (tempi changes). The horse should be able to anticipate for himself after how many strides the next change will be required. This avoids over eager, uncontrollable changing.

If the final goal is to develop flying changes after a varying number of canter strides, then it can be helpful to the horse if the trainer develops a pattern: going to the left hind side of the horse for a flying change after each second canter stride, for example, and to the right side for the flying change from stride to stride.

The Passage and the Spanish Walk

Normally, one does not begin with the passage in long reins until the horse can do this lesson reliably under the rider. For one thing, transitions from passage to extended trot encourage the horse's forward impulsion and, in expectation of this transition, the horse shows more expressive movements in the passage than without this transition, but the extended trot is not possible in long reins.

Since the prime reason for work in long reins is not exercise for the trainer but rather a means of presentation for a well-trained dressage horse with outstanding collection ability, it is important for the expressive passage under the rider to be well developed before wanting to show this in long reins.

112 *Passage in long reins: do not position your feet between the horse's hind legs—it increases the risk of being kicked.*

The same voice and hand aids as the rider uses are applied in long reins. This is why it is so important to get the horse going into the passage in response to gentle, rhythmical tongue-clicking, in reasonable tempo, with clear, trustingly accepted rein contact from hand to horse's mouth.

It is easier to motivate the horse when the desired pace is developed from a strenuous lesson such as a diligent trot in a lateral movement, or an expressive piaffe. If the horse notices that the new requirement is less strenuous, he will respond willingly. Here again, do not expect perfection to be achieved immediately. Rather it is important that the horse should receive praise even if he just shows a few slightly hesitant swinging steps. If the horse has understood what is required of him, the passage efforts can soon be extended.

With horses that have learned to do the passage by being touched on their forelegs with the whip, this method can also be applied in long reins. It should, however, be done very carefully so that the horse, under no circumstances, gets too excited and is provoked to kick out with his hind legs. Here once again, the trainer should not concentrate on the foreleg action, because this will prevent him from moving evenly with the horse, and will therefore have a generally disturbing effect.

113 The Spanish walk with a horse and a dog: not only horses can be motivated to do the Spanish walk!

In training, the passage should always be concluded after particularly expressive steps. If the horse recognizes this connection, it can have a very favorable effect on his general enthusiasm for work.

The Spanish walk in long reins can also create an impressive show effect. If the horse has already been prepared for the lesson in hand and

114 Ideal execution of the passage in long reins.

under the rider, then it will not involve any particular difficulties in long reins if the same principles are observed as were pointed out in connection with the passage. Nevertheless, particularly with the passage and the Spanish walk, one should try to constantly minimize the hand aids so that they do not become an undesirable focus of attention.

I would like to warn you against asking a horse to perform the Spanish walk in long reins too early. If forward impulsion is not absolutely confirmed, even in the difficult lessons, then the horse will always withdraw in this movement when he becomes unsure about exactly what is being required of him, or when he feels overstretched. Therefore—even at a later stage—this lesson should not be drilled as a main point of emphasis but rather it should—following preparation as described above—simply ensue as a natural happening. Also, in long reins, the basic principle applies that the horse should already be able to carry out all airs on the ground before commencing with airs above the ground.

The entire repertoire of haute école in long reins can only be achieved by a trainer who creates a positive working atmosphere and can motivate his horse to cooperate willingly even in strenuous exercises. The challenge always remains attractive and creates a particularly close relationship between trainer and horse.

Airs above the ground are elements of classical equitation, which just as the lessons of the Olympic dressage program, are part of the horse's natural behavioral pattern and, under certain conditions, can be observed in horses out at grass. Nevertheless, not every horse is equally talented for airs above the ground—this is why they cannot be made part of the standard program of a dressage test. If horses are brought on in accordance with their talents in airs above the ground, then their ability to perform can be increased as a result.

However, if these lessons are done under pressure with horses that lack talent, they have a negative effect on the horse's development and well-being.

PART FOUR
Airs Above the Ground

History

In ancient Greece, airs above the ground under the rider were already being shown for presentation purposes and also used as a means of defense in wartime riding. In the 17th and 18th centuries, they were further developed by the ennobled classes as an expression of baroque splendor and enjoyment of life, and became a form of art in their own right.

Later, for a long time, airs above the ground became restricted almost exclusively to the two important riding schools in Vienna and Saumur. The only chance to see them performed, were when presented by pupils of these institutes, and in a few highly renowned circuses. At the present time interest in such exercises is clearly increasing within the scope provided by more sophisticated leisure riding.

As they not only have a spectacular show effect, but also make a significant contribution to suppling-up and strengthening a horse, certain essential aspects will be discussed here. These can also be interesting for riders who do not intend to present airs above the ground themselves. The lessons are regularly developed in hand, and later also shown under the rider.

Equipment

Whether the horse wears side reins and is led on the cavesson, or whether these auxiliary aids are dispensed with and the horse is simply led on the snaffle or curb bit, depends on how easy it is to create a positive working atmosphere. This can normally be done more quickly with the first variation than the second.

It is essential for anyone who has difficulties in keeping his horse under control in airs above the ground to only do these under the auspices of an experienced instructor. Safety considerations are reason enough here. The following pages are therefore to be seen as an introduction into this area of equitation, and not as a conclusive discussion on the subject!

The Pesade

A preliminary exercise for the school jumps is the pesade, a raising of the forehand, which is prepared by teaching the horse to take up weight on the hind legs in the piaffe. With the correct application of the aids, the pesade can also be used as a means to an end for increasing the horse's expression in piaffe. It is important, however, that the trainer is always in a position to stipulate the horse's reactions. (Note: The pesade is steeper and therefore generally speaking, not a preliminary step to the levade. A horse that has learned to rise up steeply on the hind legs as in the pesade usually causes difficulties when asked to perform the lower-angled levade. If your ultimate goal is the levade, first review this information on pesade and then see levade on page 147.)

THE DEVELOPMENT OF THE PESADE

To prepare the horse for the pesade from a halt in a short piaffe exercise exactly on the spot, ask him to leave the ground with both forelegs at the same time by encouraging tongue-clicking in staccato (in quick succession), and a short half-halt. Apply the whip for driving purposes at the fetlocks

115 *Nardo: doing the pesade.*

116 *Marita Dreyer with her Hanoverian mare, Tina, doing the pesade in hand with such a distinct bending of the haunches that it is approaching a levade.*

of the hind legs. If the horse reacts even just very slightly, praise him liberally and reward him. Do not repeat the exercise on that day.

Not every horse reacts immediately to these aids. Nervous horses may piaffe more quickly but do not raise their forelegs from the ground. In such cases, try giving the half-halt as a surprise when already at a halt, and reinforce this immediately with staccato tongue-clicking. Some horses will rise up more easily due to the surprise effect. Then, this should be the end of the exercise for the day!

If this method does not achieve the desired effect, try, in addition to the half-halt from a halt, giving a slight slap from above on to the withers with a very short crop. Or, touch the horse's chest or forelegs with the whip. Usually this measure leads to the success desired. If not, finish the exercise, and repeat it some other day when the horse has come fresh out of the stable.

When the desired reaction takes place, the horse should then be encouraged to accept these driving aids applied to his hind fetlocks instead. It is always best to break down equitation problems into separate sections—like cutting a cake into small pieces—and to deal with them individually. In the pesade, the horse should form an angle of up to 45 degrees from the line of his back to the ground, with his forelegs drawn in. In this, compared to his position when rearing, the horse should have a good angle in the hindquarters. But do not aim for the lower position of the hindquarters until the horse has understood that he should raise both his forelegs from the ground. For this purpose, from a short piaffe exercise—the last steps with the hooves beside each other exactly on the same point—bring the whip suddenly from above to below, from the croup over the hock to the fetlock. The effect of this is that the horse comes clearly under the point of gravity with both hind legs, and thus achieves the pesade.

For these first attempts, it is important to take enough time so that the horse bends more in the haunches and does not start to rear in an uncontrolled way. The start of the pesade, the short raising of the forelegs with well-positioned

117 The differentiated application of the driving aids makes it possible to do airs above the ground without using the walls or rails of an arena as a guide: Marion Diedrich with Nardo, in a moment of the capriole.

118 *Girassol, under Ruth Giffels, in the pesade: the rider's hands positioned on the withers make it easier to handle the reins with precision.*

hindquarters, has to be absolutely controlled and succeed without any tension before the trainer should begin thinking about keeping the forehand in the air for longer.

Correct preparation also means ensuring that in raising himself, the horse under no circumstances moves backward, because this means that he comes away from the trainer's aids. This situation can be prevented by releasing the horse forward into a walk from the pesade. So here, once again, the conclusion of the collecting exercise is the "freeing forward" that maintains the horse's willingness to cooperate.

Some horses let their forelegs hang in the pesade, but the goal is for them to be well drawn in. It may surprise you to know that the remedy is in the positioning of the horse's head.

A horse's forelegs will be perfectly pulled in when the brow line (the horse's face) forms a right angle (90 degrees) with the extension of the back, or remains slightly ahead of this imaginary angle (figs. 118 and 119). By contrast, many horses let the forelegs hang because their side reins are fastened too tightly and, even in the pesade, they have to keep their brow line perpendicular to the ground. In this position, they are forced to raise their legs with a concave shaped back, which makes it impossible to pull the front legs in properly.

In addition, many horses pull in their forelegs unevenly. This mistake can be seen when the horse does not have his hind legs exactly beside each other when the forelegs are raised, but rather has one hind hoof clearly farther under the point of gravity than the other. In order to avoid this, when piaffe is used by way of preparation for raising the forelegs, it should be done exactly on the spot.

Forelegs that are brought in unevenly may also be expected when the horse is not positioned absolutely straight prior to commencing the pesade. You cannot always judge precisely from the position directly beside the horse whether this is the case or not. If you can, monitor the exercise by video, or have a competent observer with you.

Not until the horse raises his forelegs from the ground with good carriage and head position, gently and without any sense of urgency, without creeping backward, and landing just as gently again, should the horse be required to remain in the pesade position—for up to four seconds and longer. Use the staccato tongue-clicking for the introduction of the pesade and, at the same time, give finely vibrating half-halts.

If the horse unintentionally offers pesades of his own accord, first of all check whether or not your aids are clear. In particular, the trainer

119 *The pesade performed in the Herrenhaus Gardens, Hannover.*

should not even think about the pesade while a horse is carrying out another lesson. If the horse nevertheless presents pesades without the relevant request being made, these should be ignored and the horse gently corrected by asking for a longer interval of piaffe.

If this also has no effect, ask the horse that offers undesired pesades to do exaggeratedly long periods of raised (individual) forelegs so that a pesade is made difficult and the horse no longer offers them of his own accord.

The Pesade Under Saddle

If the horse does the pesade in hand in a well-controlled way, then the trainer may allow a rider to sit on the horse with the rider remaining inactive at first and taking care not to upset the horse with faults in the seat. She should look at something at eye-level in order to keep a feeling for the vertical position of her upper body during the raising of the forehand. If the rider looks down to the ground and if her body comes in front of the vertical, then she will make it difficult for the horse to do this balancing act.

Exact balancing on the spot with well pulled-in forelegs has a higher priority than keeping the horse in the levade for a particularly long time (over four seconds), although a long-lasting levade is extremely fascinating for the rider as well as for the spectators.

Gradually, the rider takes over the aids for the pesade by staccato tongue-clicking as well as driving with her legs, keeping good contact with the reins to achieve increased stepping under of the hind legs, and a raising of the forelegs from the ground. It is not until the landing that the hands, which, particularly in the first attempts, are positioned on the withers for a calming effect, go slightly forward in order to release the horse from the pesade into the walk. If the horse has not made enough effort, then piaffe should be done again immediately and the next pesade prepared.

The trainer, who accompanies this on foot, may gradually decrease his influence. In the initial period he can have a calming effect and, if the horse has balancing difficulties, he can pull the leading rein gently downward to prevent the horse from rising too steeply. In my experience, following correct preparation, the rider can carry out pesades without help from the ground within a very short time.

Successful pesades are exceptionally beautiful to look at

120 *In the levade: the Andalusian stallion, Divertido, with distinct bending of the haunches.*

and are not just for preparation of the school jumps; they are also a means to improve the upward action of the horse in piaffe. This lesson is not just a goal in itself, but can, in a variety of different contexts, be a means to an end.

The Levade

In the levade, the horse is positioned low in the haunches, with just a very slight raising of the back into an angle of up to 35 degrees from the ground, with both forelegs pulled in evenly. At the beginning, the hind feet come under the center of gravity with the hocks coming lower to the ground so that, with horses that can do the levade particularly well, one has the impression that they become larger at the end of the exercise in the transition to the walk or the halt. The ideal levade thus requires a much more powerful horse than the pesade and cannot be expected from every horse.

Quality features are, in addition to the strongly angled hind legs and just slight slant of the back, a gentle "raising" and good pulling-in of the forelegs that is almost unnoticeable for the rider, as well as a gentle stepping-off of the forelegs at the end of the levade. Once again, after this lesson, the horse should be released forward into the walk in order to prevent any undesired creeping backward.

Exact balancing on the spot with well pulled-in forelegs has a higher priority than keeping the horse in the levade for a particularly long time (over four seconds), although a long-lasting levade is extremely fascinating for the rider as well as for the spectators.

THE DEVELOPMENT OF THE LEVADE

The levade is developed in hand, like the pesade from a deeply set piaffe with the last steps being done on the spot. It is particularly important to only demand a few piaffe steps out of the halt in the initial period—with a fast lowering of the whip from the croup to the fetlocks. In preparing the levade it is essential that the horse be optimally positioned within these few piaffe steps if he is not to become exhausted before drawing in the forelegs. In such a case there is a danger that, as a result of fear of the demand imposed, the horse will react with uncontrolled, nervous steps.

A trainer should be satisfied with just practicing the beginning of the levade over a lengthy period of time. Long practice of the correct beginning strengthens the horse for "standing" in the levade, which is what we are aiming for later. The levade is really only correct when the horse does not creep backward and the topline remains close to the horizontal. If you ask too much, too early, you will not achieve success: an ideal levade cannot be forced!

THE LEVADE UNDER SADDLE

If the levade in hand succeeds, prepare for it under the rider in a similar way to the pesade. A major feature here is a stronger positioning of the hindquarters and just a slightly rising topline. The horse's balancing act is, under no circumstances, to be disturbed by the rider. To introduce the levade, the rider puts his legs back slightly and ensures that he remains sitting vertically throughout the entire levade. He must not come ahead of the vertical, or go behind it with the upper part of his body.

The horse becomes lower behind the rider, while at the front he comes slightly nearer to the rider's upper body with

his head and neck. At the same time, the area of the horse's back under the rider's seat continues to swing gently, almost at the same level as before in the piaffe—an indescribable feeling!

121 *The courbette presented in extended style.*

The Courbette

The courbette that is performed today has been modified from its original form in order to increase its attractiveness.

In the courbette, as it is shown in Vienna, the horse jumps forward with raised forelegs and lands again on the hind legs. A horse experienced in courbettes can do a series of them without landing on the forelegs. The courbette described in this section is according to the style practiced at Saumur.

The Development of the Courbette

A prerequisite for the courbette is a well-balanced pesade. From this, the horse, initially in hand, is asked to jump forward in response to a light touching of the hind legs above the hock. Vibrating, light rein pulls encourage the horse to stay in the air with the forehand until the hind feet have land-

122 *Nardo: doing the preliminary stage of the courbette.*

ed. Praise and reward the horse! It is best initially to do courbettes in hand with two people. Attach the longe to the outside of the cavesson or bridle to keep the horse straight and to support the upward tendency of the forehand.

If the horse has understood that he should do a step forward on the hind legs, then he can be asked to remain in a pesade to give the horse a feeling of the forward and upward tendency. If this combination succeeds with light aids, then the trainer can aim for a second leap without an interim landing on the forehand. This usually only succeeds when the first courbette is not done too high and does not cover too much ground: only when the leaps are conducted energetically, but at the same time short and flat, is there a chance of achieving an exceptionally high number of leaps in succession before the horse needs to land on the forehand. The energetic execution of the leaps makes them look high and broad.

The trainer must not simply aim for a large number of leaps. Four leaps are already an exceptional performance. Only very few horses are in a position to gradually reach a level where they can do considerably more leaps.

When developing the training, always remember that the number of leaps is by no means the only quality feature of the courbette. Rather, the lesson should be so harmonious that even for the rider sitting on the horse, it does not represent a

safety risk. In particular, pay attention to the fact that the horse's topline does not become too steep in the courbette, as this would increase the danger of the horse rolling over backward.

THE COURBETTE UNDER SADDLE

For reasons of safety and aesthetics, pay particular attention to ensure that the horse is well balanced, and that he does not storm forward without being regulated appropriately. For this, the rider asks his horse to jump into the courbette from the pesade with rein-forced driving aids—initially with support from the ground—and, by means of gentle but clear half-halts, delays a landing of the forehand. If you really want to show several leaps in succession, always let your horse go back into the pesade between leaps. A particularly impressive

124 *Even in difficult lessons, aim for a performance without constraint: Maggie in the courbette.*

125 Preparation for the capriole.

example of this was given by the First Chief Rider of the Spanish Riding School in Vienna, Ignaz Lauscha, on his bay Lippizan stallion, Siglavy Flora, who always did his fourth leap as a pesade in order to continue a sequence of leaps up to a twelfth leap without his front legs ever touching the ground.

Despite the pleasure created by such exceptional performances, it should be remembered that such work is only to be strived for with particularly talented and powerful horses. Any other horses will simply be ruined by the attempt.

The Capriole

In the capriole, the horse jumps from a raised position of the forehand into the air, kicks out with the hind legs—"stretches"—and lands more or less on all four legs at the same time. This effort requires powerful, well-balanced horses that can be well regulated in the piaffe and pesade, and show an obvious tendency for being able to kick out in response to a crack with the whiplash, or touching on the croup with the whip.

A capriole, conducted correctly in hand or under the

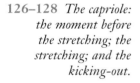

126–128 The capriole: the moment before the stretching; the stretching; and the kicking-out.

rider, has a suppling-up effect similar to loose jumping—for advanced riders who are prepared to depart from conventional paths, it represents a particularly attractive goal on the way to suppling-up and collecting. Even when you are concentrating on fine technical details, pay attention to lightness in this difficult lesson.

An outstanding example here is the present First Chief Rider of the Spanish Riding School in Vienna, Arthur Kottas-Heldenberg, with the best capriole horse of the 20th century, Conversano Valdamora, who can perform perfect caprioles and then land on the diagonals in the passage and continue the line in the right rhythm. In doing this, horse and rider radiate the harmony of a work of art, and are accepted enthusiastically by spectators. The thought of such performances may encourage talented riders, not simply to stand still in awe and admiration, but rather to take up the exciting challenge of further reviving the elements of classical equitation!

THE DEVELOPMENT OF THE CAPRIOLE

In hand, encourage the horse to kick out with his head positioned low. Normally, a helper leads the horse wearing side reins. The trainer follows at an appropriate distance and drives with the whip while holding a longe rein that runs over the withers into the outside cavesson or snaffle ring. If the

kicking-out works in response to subtle aids, the horse can come out of the piaffe or the collected canter to a courbette leap and, by means of a small crack of the whip or touching of the croup with the whip, be asked to stretch and kick.

Particularly in the initial period, be satisfied with little, and praise a lot even if the result is not yet perfect.

It is difficult to get the horse to stretch at just the right moment: if the aid comes too early, some horses do not stretch at all, but rather just jump forward; if it comes too late, the horse does not stretch until he has already landed with the front feet.

To avoid causing the horse to invest energy in the wrong direction, take care that he does not slowly rise to the pesade and then balance in it, because then there is usually too little strength left for the desired leap. Rather, from the preparing movement, by means of tongue-clicking and a pull on the outside rein, bring the horse to jump off quickly because this increases the chances of success for still stretching in the upward movement.

129 Barbie Jung with the Lipizzaner, Favory X Capra, in the capriole.

THE CAPRIOLE UNDER SADDLE

Only a horse that stretches early enough gives the rider a pleasant "sitting" feeling later on: if he stretches too late and lands on the front hooves first and considerably later on the hind hooves, this is always hard on the rider. At the beginning, the rider should have help from below, just as with other airs above the ground: from the piaffe or the collected canter, the upper part of the body should be taken back somewhat, thus driving the horse into stronger rein contact. Together with encouraging tongue-clicking, introduce the raising of the forehand. If the contact is not firm, this could mean that the horse disobeys and the forehand remains on the ground.

Ask for the leap by firmly closing the legs. At first, the person on the ground should give the aid to stretch with a touch of the whip: the trainer on foot can better estimate the right moment for the aids from his position. These are the aids that the horse already knows from his work in hand and reacts to without hesitation. Later on, the rider can use the whip himself to ask the horse to kick out.

130 *The finishing phase of the capriole.*

There are horses that develop the tendency to just stretch on the side on which they are touched with the whip, and to let the hind leg on the other side hang down. They can be corrected by riding for a time with two whips and applying the aid to stretch alternately, sometimes on the right side and on the next capriole on the left side. This increases the horse's willingness to kick out.

Epilogue

NEW POSSIBILITIES!

In lessons and at presentations, riders often tell me that my way of working with horses is new for them. Thus the video, as a supplement to this book, can be of practical assistance to readers who have not actually seen the work being done and who would also like to embark on new methods in the training of their horses.

The video does not always show the ideal execution of certain lessons, but rather attracts attention to difficulties in dealing with the horse and possible ways of solving such problems. Not all of these suggestions will be practical for every reader to enforce.

The videotape and book should, however, help more people to become aware of the fact that there are different methods within the system of classical equitation that can lead to success, independent of the character of the trainer and the horse. Every trainer should explore the applications of these methods without prejudice—in their own interest as well as the interest of the horse.

Index

Page numbers in *italics* indicate illustrations.